Text
Kevin Jackson

Photography
Richard Heeps

fast

feasting
on the streets
of London

Portobello
BOOKS

Published by
Portobello Books Ltd 2006

Portobello Books Ltd
Eardley House
4 Uxbridge Street
Notting Hill Gate
London W8 7SY
UK

A CIP catalogue record is available
from the British Library

9 8 7 6 5 4 3 2 1

ISBN 1-84627-029-4

www.portobellobooks.com

Designed by Mr & Mrs Smith

Printed and bound in China by
Compass Press

In memory of Tom Cocklin, actor and writer

PALM'S CAFE

BREWER STREET, SOHO

In the early hours of 17 May 1998, one of the most famous Englishmen of his day, the gifted if erratic footballer Paul Gascoigne — 'Gazza' — came in search of some tasty blotter after one of his regular drinking sessions with a couple of pals, the laddish DJs Danny Baker and Chris Evans. An amateur photographer, James Eison, happened to be passing, and he took an im-promptu snap of the munching revellers — a serious embarrassment for Gazza, since he was in training for the England World Cup squad, and had promised to be in bed, sober, by mid-night every night. So the three loutish celebrities seized Eison's camera and threw it under the wheels of a passing car. The camera was ruined, but the film was rescued. Every tabloid in the country ran the picture of lagered-up Gazza, brandishing an incriminating object: a chicken kebab. A kebab!

Its significance would, no doubt, have been quite lost on French, American or Taiwanese tourists, but none of the red-top editorialists needed to explain the sordid connotations of Gazza's culinary choice to a chuckling nation. For 25 years or more, the kebab has been acknowledged as Britain's yob-fodder supreme: hurled down at two or three in the morning by gangs of pissed, white oiks who, as often as not, then hurl it up again on the pavement; greasy, grey-brown slivers of pounded fat and gristle, no doubt throbbing with evil bacteria (the classic doner kebab), or cauterized chunks of chewy meat, provenance uncertain, made marginally edible only by lavish, mouth-numbing doses of napalm-strength chilli sauce; the whole confection served up in a bland bread pocket guaranteed to fall apart seconds after receiving its squidgy contents, and garnished with cheap salad stuff — a perfunctory gesture towards healthy eating which the oafish cognoscenti usually discard into the gutter.

No other contemporary foodstuff, not even the sphincter-punishing vindaloo, so immediately brands its consumer as a dietary hooligan. For Gazza, it was the gourmandizing equivalent of being caught with a pound of heroin in his hand. Worse, probably, since heroin addicts at least tend to be skinny, and the footballer's struggles to stave off his chronic chubbiness were as notorious as his penchant for bursting into tears when things went awry on the field of play. The England manager, Glenn Hoddle, waxed pious about the Great Kebab Scandal and promptly dropped Gascoigne from the squad. His career died, you might say, of fast-food poisoning.

The Palm's Cafe, however, did quite well out of the incident. They marketed a 'Gazza Kebab' at £3. It sold briskly.

KING'S KEBAB HOUSE
EARLS COURT

Ignore every harsh word I have just written about the noble kebab, Turkey's finest gift to the rest of humanity. Properly done, with good-quality ingredients, it is one of the most reliable consolations of a carnivore's existence.

This chicken kebab, for instance, freshly prepared for me by the proprietor of King's Kebab House, Mr Mughal. Even the warm pitta bread is a minor treat — brittle and abrasive at the extremities where the grill has lightly scorched it, agreeably pulpy and yielding inside. These complementary textures are echoed by the small chicken pieces, brown and gently resistant on the outside, soft and white and running with clear, succulent juices within. Lettuce and tomato add freshness and sweetness, mild vinegared jalapenos and lemon juice a zesty tang, and the traditional chilli sauce is just the right intensity, hot enough to present a mild challenge to the palate, gentle enough not to

obliterate the more subtle flavours. A garlic sauce — unusual addition — gives the mouthful a satisfyingly protracted 'finish', as wine writers call that slow fading sensation on the taste buds.

As a one-course meal, it is just about perfect, and I defy any killjoy nutritionist to tell me that eating it has set me on a slow course to suicide. Nor am I likely to have my athletic career — or even my aesthetic one — ruined if anyone spots me. But then, I am sitting down at a table and eating my kebab quietly, in a state of sobriety and in daylight hours, not staggering down a street at 3a.m. It illustrates just about the oldest, most elementary rule of cultural anthropology: Context Confers Meaning.

Such musings are prompted, in part, by the preliminary discussions I've been having with my partner in this mission, the photographer Richard Heeps, ever since we were first commissioned to go for — how exactly to term it? — a wander, a mooch, a ramble, a meander, a *dérive* around London's fast food joints. The point is not to produce another diatribe in the

tradition of *Fast Food Nation* (much as I approve of Eric Schlosser's book), but to winkle out something of what it all looks and feels and, yes, smells and tastes like to eat on the hoof on the streets of London.

We have decided to start our journey (a) in Earls Court, since Kangaroo Valley was one of the earliest of London's districts to attract such outlets in bulk in the post-war period ('You can have a hamburger *à l'anglaise* at the Wimpy bar in the Earls Court Road, open all night,' notes one suitably impressed contributor to Len Deighton's *London Dossier*, 1967), and (b) in a kebab shop, since Gazza's favourite middle-eastern import is now as integral a part of British food culture as . . . well, as the curry house. Ah, the curry house: a well-loved, invaluable and fascinating institution which, I suggested to Richard, sadly tends to fall outside our immediate brief, as usually being too much like a traditional restaurant. Same goes for a lot of Chinese, Thai and other Asian restaurants.

So what exactly are we calling 'fast food', then? Tricky question. It would take a St Thomas Aquinas to come up with a definition of 'fast food' that would gratify every pedant. Again, in many instances it is a straightforward case of CCM: Context Confers Meaning. Pizza is a fast food if you buy it from a van or in a Pizza Hut, but a main course in a trattoria or *ristorante*; burgers are fast food from the place with the Golden Arches, but a moderately pricey meal washed down with a robust red in a Tootsie's; spicy fried chicken a Confederate nostalgist's delight in a Manhattan theme restaurant such as (the late, lamented) Beulah and down-home soul food in Harlem, but neither of those things at a KFC.

Economics isn't the whole story, either. Although fast food tends to be reasonably cheap or even dirt cheap, at the global level price is no longer an infallible indicator of fast food status: in some of McDonald's newer markets (Beijing, say), it is precisely the fact that the product is satisfyingly expensive, readily affordable only to yuppies, that makes conspicuous chomping on a Big Mac such a fantasy-charged experience. Even the apparently self-evident 'fast-ness' isn't an entirely trustworthy criterion, at any rate when it comes to the consumer:

though the average American customer of McDonald's will finish a meal within eleven minutes, customers in Korea may stay two hours, three hours or even longer, treating the air-conditioned restaurants as unofficial youth clubs or places of refuge from family tensions.

Perhaps we could start negatively, and work towards some handy rules of thumb with the observation that the local tandoori place, like other traditional restaurants, will usually boast several features that fast food joints often or generally lack: waiter service rather than counter service, tipping, tablecloths, alcoholic drinks ('I think that I shall never hear / A poem fine as Cobra Beer . . .'), proper glassware, proper cutlery, proper napkins . . . and, one could add, proper cooking, rather than an industrial process of warming prefabricated food units. Where those grace notes are missing, we're on the right track.

So, apart from kebabs, are we really just talking about McDonald's, Pizza Hut, Burger King and KFC? No, not just those. Most commentators on fast food, especially the Jeremiahs, speak of the phenomenon as though it were wholly a question of globalism and US imperialism — of the giant chains conquering Britain precisely as they have conquered dozens of other nations (in the case of McDonald's: 121 other countries at last count, a notable exception being Sierra Leone), with devastating effects on indigenous waistlines and dental health, labour practices and table etiquette. Not to mention the larger-scale misgivings about global agriculture and the environment. The present-day fast food scare amongst *bien-pensant* intellectuals is cold war paranoia in mirror image: instead of the (right-wing) Domino Theory, the (left-wing) Domino's Pizza Theory.

Now, the main force of such *No Logo* arguments — well outlined in *Fast Food Nation* and amusingly dramatized in the muck-raking documentary *Supersize Me* (2004) — will only be denied by scoundrels, shareholders, CEOs and other interested parties. As a neo-Ruskinian who had literally not set foot inside a McDonald's outlet for about eighteen years before undertaking this mission, I am very largely in sympathy with the argument that such places are not merely tacky but abominations. But, hang on a moment, comrades, and listen to the wisdom of the world's most eminent anthropologist of sugar production and consumption:

'While the eating of great quantities of food imported from remote regions only began to be typical of world diet after the seventeenth century, eating the equivalent of what is now called "fast food" has been a feature of human food behaviour for millennia.' (Sidney W. Mintz, *Swallowing Modernity*, 1997)

Though it is often assumed or asserted or argued that fast food is one of the distinctive and garish features of modernity, known only since the 1950s or so — that is, when the methods of factory production entered the restaurant industry in California and then other parts of the USA — impartial rumination on the facts leads one to believe that Mintz's position is pretty much unassailable. To speak of 'fast food' from previous epochs — as, say, the historian Martha Carlin does in her essay *Provisions for the Poor: Fast Food in Medieval London* (1999) — is not to proffer one of those sickly exercises in anachronism which telly historians and pandering school teachers use to make their subject seem 'relevant', but to articulate a demonstrable and sometimes harsh truth. By this broader definition, fast food has been the immemorial diet of the urban poor (as opposed to the peasantry).

Don't look at the technology of production, look at who's spending the pennies and testrils and farthings:

'Large numbers of Londoners were for centuries compelled by the circumstances of their lives or daily routines to rely on street traders for at least part of their diet. Labourers working on building sites or along the riverside constituted a ready market, as did the meat-porters at Smithfield who sustained the cookshops of nearby Pye Corner. The multiple occupancy of former grand houses condemned many to rooms without access to a proper kitchen. Tens of thousands more were lodgers with families who might not care, or be able, to feed them . . .' (Richard Tames, *Feeding London*, 2003)

This is the ugly, unpalatable side of the story. A happier, or at any rate livelier, picture is made by the spectacle of the countless small-scale institutions which sprang up across the centuries to serve this ragged army of citizens without a kitchen. Coffee shops, ordinaries, inns, taverns and pie shops (hello, Sweeney Todd!), Lyons Corner Houses and ABCs, street vendors of oysters and hot potatoes and pies and fruits and pottage, and later of cockles and whelks and coffee and buns. Small and larger waves of immigration since the early Victorian period, from Italy, Eastern Europe, from China, from the Indian sub-continent, from the West Indies and from Greece and Turkey have all helped enlarge the range of metropolitan street fare . . . and, thus, considerably to mitigate the homogenizing tendencies of the American giants, who only started to arrive here quite recently, in the early 1970s. The first UK McDonald's opened as recently as 1974.

Besides the ubiquitous kebab joint, London's present-day fast food panorama includes the neighbourhood fish and chip shop, the vegan takeaway, a few stubbornly surviving jellied eel stalls, the local caff which will do you a nice hot sausage sandwich and a plastic cup of weak, sugary tea to go, the Jamaica patty or Cornish pasty stand, the neatly arranged sushi boxes from Pret A Manger or Sainsbury's or Marks & Sparks, the calorie-counting snacks from Boots the chemists, the railway and tube station buffets, the itinerant hot dog vendors, the rib joints, the weirdly named spicy fried chicken emporia of the outer suburbs which pay no franchise dues to the famous Southern Colonel, and their no less oddly named counterparts in the business of rapid-delivery pizza, the ever-reliable baguettes from Upper Crust, the thriving Starbucks (US culinary imperialism, yuppie division) and Costas and other overpriced coffee shops, the juice bars, the vending trolleys on main-line trains, the soggy and tightly wrapped and all but tasteless white-bread sandwiches sold by garages and newsagents, the ice cream vans, the assorted outlets for smoothies and the vegetable samosas ('would you like that heated up?'), the independent burger bars and the short-lived, niche-marketed speciality chains like Soup Opera (recently deceased) . . . and the Wimpy Bar.

These are the sorts of place in which Richard and I will be pottering around. And the King's Kebab House proves to be a lucky place to begin, not only because their food is good but because they welcome our presence. After a little early negotiating, that is. Mr Mughal asks me to make a phone call to the owner for permission to photograph. 'How much will it cost me?' asks the suspicious voice down the line. When I explain the nature of our mission a little more clearly, permission is granted.

Like many such establishments, the King's Kebab House is run as a family business. (In the major fast food chains — let's call them McWorld, for short — not only are the staff members generally unrelated, but in many cases the turnaround in work crews is so frequent that there's not much point in fostering workplace friendships.) Usually, the family would be Turkish — in fact, so many Turkish people are involved in London's fast food industry that one suspects that half our restaurants would vanish overnight if the capital's Turks suddenly yielded to mass homesickness and went back to Ankara or Istanbul.

Mr Mughal and his family are from Pakistan — Londoners don't seem too fussed about ethnic authenticity when it comes to their grub — but they take as much pride in their Middle-Eastern fare as any restaurateurs from the Levant. Indeed, this is the only kebab shop I've ever seen where the display tray of hummus has been carefully groomed with a fork and garnished with cucumber slices so that it looks like a miniature Zen garden. And the three rotating spits — one doner, one chicken, one lamb — are topped with mock-floral arrangements, improvised from onions, lemons and tomatoes. The Mughal family have been in the restaurant business for 27 years, and have run this place for the last three. They say that there has been a kebab shop on these premises since 1947 — which, if true, would surely make this one of the oldest kebab places in London? Anecdotal evidence, based on asking those aged 50 and over, suggests that kebabs were still something of a novelty until the late 1960s or early 1970s.

Manze's

Eels

Small jellied Eels	3 – 00	
large " "	6 – 00	
Small Hot Eels	3 – 00	
large Hot Eels	6 – 00	
Hot Eels & Mash	4 – 00	
large Hot Eels & Mash	7 – 00	

Cold
Hot
large
Fruit
Mash
Carton
ladle of

Business is slow at lunchtime, and probably won't pick up until the early evening; the House advertises that it stays open every morning until 5a.m., and so it once did, but since the World Trade Center atrocities, Mr Mughal says, custom has fallen off sharply and nowadays they'll often close for the night by 1a.m. Whatever the London tourist authorities are saying, you just don't see as many hungry Americans and Australians around here as before; not so many Arabs, either. I say that I hope the minor publicity of being in our book will give business a little fillip. Mr Mughal gives us both a warm, two-fisted handshake as we leave. I notice that they are selling a soft drink called 'Rubicon' (60p a can, 70p a carton) and just about manage to resist telling Richard that we have now crossed the Rubicon. Smart-arse remarks like that irritate him.

→

Kebab snobbery reprised at **City Kebab House**, *p.64*

SNAPPY TOMATO PIZZA
EARLS COURT

Kebabs, pizza, fish and chips . . . the idea for the first few days of our odyssey is to check out all three of these 'British' treats before tapping into McWorld. The anthropologist James L. Watson recently drew up a shortlist of the world's principal fast foods and their points of national origin:

roughly:

UK	fish and chips
China	noodles
Japan	station box lunches (*ekibento*)
Turkey	street kebabs
Germany	sausage and bread – hot dogs (but see below)
USA	burgers, fried chicken pieces

The list plainly howls out for amendment, if only by:

France/ Belgium	French fries aka chips (but see below)
UK	sandwiches

But today I am keenest to add:

Italy	ice cream, pizza

Snappy Tomato Pizza is typical of all those independents who are fighting the American leaders, Pizza Hut and Domino's, for a slice (pun unpremeditated) of the Italianate savoury open-pie market. They don't run to a salad bar, but if you feel like something other than a pizza they also offer jalapeno peppers (£2.75), loaded potato skins (£2.50 for cheese, £2.99 for cheese and bacon), garlic mushrooms (£2.99) or chicken nuggets (£2.20); their delivery service is free.

Again, business is slow this hot, sunny, early afternoon. The head pizza cook, Mario Leite (he comes from Brazil, not Italy), passes the empty time with a display of old-fashioned kitchen skill for our benefit. He tosses discs of pizza dough in the air, catches them on the tips of his fingers, spins them like a Frisbee so that they grow wider and wider, thinner and thinner, and eventually are flat enough to have cheese and sauces smeared across them, ready for the oven. If he spins them for too long, they split in the middle, and have to be mashed back into balls, then rolled again into discs.

Mario is a bright guy, full of quips, a natural performer for the camera. He says that he has been in the pizza business for ten years. Let not ambition mock his useful toil, but one cannot help but think him cut out for more creative work.

More molten mozarella at **Chicken Village Pizza**, *p.63*

FISH AND CHIPS (AKA 'SEASONS')
GLOUCESTER ROAD

'If this means negative publicity, I'm coming after you,' the manager warns us, only half joking. No call for alarm, sir: this is plainly a well-run, top-of-the-scale chippy, clean and bright and reasonably priced, and the fish and chips themselves have a seductive golden glow as they're lifted from the seething oil. 'Excellent food,' mutters Richard, who's been allowed behind the counter, and is trying for some extreme close-ups that will do justice to the sight. If I wasn't already full of chicken kebab, I'd probably see off a plateful of haddock in no time flat.

Unlike the fish and chip shops of my South London childhood in the 1960s, which were usually little more than serving counters and maybe a couple of seats in the back, 'Seasons' is a large, high-ceilinged open-plan room with plenty of chromium tables inside and out. The staff wear neat blue T-shirts advertising 'Shark', a soft drink, and baseball caps greeting the customer with 'Salut!' Pop music fills the air — 'Can't Get You Out of My Head' by Kylie, 'Naughty Girl' by Beyoncé — and sometimes makes the swift movements of the work crew seem almost choreographed. All the staff are too busy to be interviewed, so I can just sip my mineral water and muse at leisure while Richard does the proper work.

→

An archaeology of fish and chips at
Burned-Out, p.52

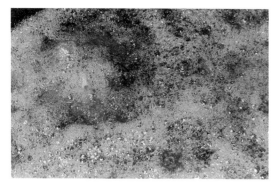

ON FISH AND CHIPS AND OTHER DIGITAL FOOD

The most searching essay I know on fish and chips was written by Gilbert Adair, and published in his collection *Myths and Memories*. It's a self-conscious reprisal of a famous, much-cited essay on steak and chips by Roland Barthes in *Mythologies*. Barthes argues, among other things, for the function of steak and chips as a potent signifier of quintessential Frenchness, and particularly of Frenchness in its more virile mode. Adair proposes, with (to my mind) greater wit and resourcefulness, that Fish and Chips, or fish'n'chips, performs the same function — and others besides — for the United Kingdom.

It's certainly hard to imagine a punter entirely innocent of at least one symbolic dimension of the dish. In Benidorm — and yes, cynical reader, I have honestly observed this at first hand — tourist restaurants advertise their meals of fish and chips and the all-day British Breakfast with large

Union Jack motifs: a simultaneous appeal to purity of palate (no oily, garlicky, foreign muck here), to safety (no frightening tentacles or gizzards), to nostalgia and comfort (food just like Mum used to buy) and to pig-headed patriotism (why should we change what we usually eat just because we're in Spain?). The mentality here is simultaneously aggressive and regressive . . . but then, since it would be a weird British holidaymaker who came to Benidorm mainly for the cuisine, there wouldn't be much mileage in pointing out that a short walk along the beach will take you to a part of town where very good Spanish food is cheaply and plentifully available.

Am I being snobbish? Well, obviously. Hard not to be, when the foodstuff in question is also so firmly bound up in class allegiances as well as national ones. A recent Anglo-American movie, *51st State*, included a scene in which the visiting American character, played by the charismatic Samuel L. Jackson, comes to England and is introduced to fish and chips as the national dish. 'This ain't a national dish,' he says, incredulous and disgusted, 'this is a national disaster.' But the quip is ill-targeted: fish and chips is really the totemic dish, not of Britons in general, but of Britain's industrial working classes. Hence the misfired insult in an episode of *Cheers*, in which a posh English psychiatrist (played by John Cleese) is sneered at as a 'sack of fish and chips'. The old French culinary insult, *'le rosbif'*, would have been far closer to the point.

Although almost everyone likes the product (it's not like the kind of painful *nostalgie de la boue* that would be in play if one called for such doubtfully edible childhood/prole horrors as spam sandwiches or Waggon Wheels or Pot Noodles or deep-fried Mars Bars), there is a faint but inescapable tang of slumming when members of the bourgeoisie or gentry order fish'n'chips; rich people sometimes turn their unwontedly cheap meal into a little sumptuary joke by washing it down with champagne instead of tea, Tizer or beer. Plain, old-fashioned slumming, or, at other times, that slightly queasy affectation of being a no-nonsense man or woman of the people which you can also detect when a politician of the claret-swilling classes conspicuously orders and drinks a pint of bitter for the benefit of the cameras.

For some, then, eating fish and chips represents a temporary adjustment of class habits; for others, a pleasurable, even blissful return to childhood joys. A visit to the chip shop, whether for a full-blown meal or the greedy snack of a few pennyworth of chips served up with stingingly sour pickled onions, was the most reliable boyhood treat of all, indulged in with my mother about once a week or so. (My father had been turned off fish by his experiences in the army, where it was often served half-rotten; it took him some four decades to overcome his learned disgust.) As today, cod and chips was probably the most frequently ordered meal, but there were other forms of deep-fried seafood which are now all but unknown, as a result either of depleted fish stocks or changes in taste.

If memory serves: at the luxury end of the scale, a little more expensive than other fish, was skate — nowadays not nearly so common outside fancy fish restaurants. At the cheapest end, costing just a few pence, little battered cakes of cod roe: pink-brown on the inside, crumbly on the tongue, stronger-tasting than the classic fishcake, which was essentially a bland white mush eked out with spud and flecked with parsley. Between the two, and a frequent alternative to cod, was so-called 'rock salmon', a type of dogfish, which had a single thick, soft, semi-translucent bone running through it; the final stage of consumption was to suck the bone dry, removing every last flake of white flesh. Most chip shops would serve saveloys — oversized sausages, with softer and spicier meat than your standard banger (see below) — and some would serve pease pudding, a fibrous yellow dish largely unchanged since the middle ages. One of the small but distinct pleasures of fish and chips eaten in the street was precisely the same as that which is now experienced by everyone who buys a hamburger, a pizza slice or a bucket of fried chicken: you were allowed, indeed encouraged, to eat it with your fingers. A small pronged piece of wood, halfway between a spoon and a fork, was provided for those with delicate digits. You still see them here and there, and Bill Bailey refers to them in his spot-on parody of Billy Bragg, 'Unisex Chip Shop': 'I carved her name, Debbie, on a little wooden fork . . .'

This business of the atavistic delight of eating with the fingers is an under-examined aspect of the fast food world, though a study of the impact of McDonald's in Japan (by the anthropologist Emiko Ohnuki-Tierney) did establish that the arrival of burgers had introduced the practice of eating without chopsticks to a culture which had always regarded direct finger contact with all but a very limited range of foods — such as *nigirizushi*, vinegared rice balls with raw fish — as both impolite and unhygienic. To this day, sharp-eyed observers report, you will see young girls in Tokyo carefully using the grease-proof paper of the burger packaging as a protective barrier between fingers and bun. Eating at McDonald's has also considerably weakened the taboo against eating when standing, *tachigui*. A well-known Japanese novelist of the early twentieth century, Nagai Kafu, wrote a series of stories, *Amerika Monogatari* (1908), in which he shudderingly characterized Chicago as 'the place where people grab food and eat while standing'. But the first McDonald's opened in Tokyo had no seating . . . Finger food, to digress just a little further, invites us to cast off some of the basic training which took us from babyhood to childhood; or, in the broader historical sense, to cast off that gradual development of a refined mealtime etiquette, of which a major turning point came around the reign of Richard II, who appears to have been the first English monarch to encourage the use of a fancy gadget from Italy known as the fork. The sociologist Norbert Elias has told some of this story in *The Civilizing Process, Vol. I: The History of Manners*, 1939:

'Why is it "barbaric" and "uncivilized" to put food into one's mouth by hand from one's own plate? Because it is distasteful to dirty one's fingers, or at least to be seen in society with dirty fingers. The suppression of eating by hand from one's own plate has very little to do with the danger of illness, the so-called "rational" explanation. In observing our feelings toward the fork ritual, we can see with particular clarity that the first authority in our decision between "civilized" and "uncivilized" behavior at table is our feeling of distaste. The fork is nothing other than the embodiment of a specific standard of emotions and a specific level of revulsion.' ('On the Use of the Fork at Table')

A well-known English novelist of the later twentieth century, Anthony Burgess (who had experienced the exquisitely refined cuisines of Malaysia and Italy, as well as the robust fare of his native Manchester), once wrote that fish and chips, eaten directly from the wrapping paper on the street, was the finest food in the world. At the age of eight, I would have agreed with him heartily: the food seemed to taste particularly good when eaten at night in cold, damp weather, and above all in the pouring rain, though you had to be careful not to let your chips get soggy and your tangy malt vinegar diluted.

The symbolic end of that popular gastronomic era came in 1968, when the Ministry of Health banned the sale of fish and chips wrapped in newspaper. To this day, there are people who will swear to you that it tasted better when served up in stories of transvestites and naughty vicars. Despite this spoilsport move, the National Union of Journalists long continued to send an annual greeting to the Federation of Fish Friers: 'Your trade is wrapped up in ours.'

GRAB A BITE
GLOUCESTER ROAD UNDERGROUND STATION

An unusual sight: Gloucester Road is one of the comparatively few stations in central London which has tracks that run on either side of the platform; uncomfortable for anyone who suffers from the Imp of the Perverse, and hears a little demon voice yelling 'jump!' as the train pulls in. The Grab a Bite stand is located right on the platform, and almost begs to be photographed.

Nadya and Amit, working the late afternoon shift, are happy to pose, and obligingly stay rock-still while Richard takes long-exposure shots of the trains pulling into and out of the platforms. A visual play with ideas of fastness: here the commuters are fast, but the foodstuffs are motionless as any stone.

PORTOBELLO ROAD CAFE
NOTTING HILL

We are drawn to the interior by a colourful mural, a wall-sized cartoon, suitably goofy and lurid, of the street vista you can see through the cafe's front window. Two local men, in their seventies or thereabouts, are here for a snack and some fizzy drink and an afternoon chat, as is their daily habit — Albert Taylor and Stanley Carpenter. Albert, who's never lived more than about half a mile or so from this spot, is particularly interested by our business: 'Are you making a documentary?' he asks, mistaking Richard's portrait camera for the movie type. 'You could call it "The Characters of the Caff". Or how about "Two of the Layabouts on Portobello Road"? I like that . . . got a ring to it.'

He continues to chat as Richard takes shot after shot, waxing increasingly surprised at how slow and painstaking a business it is, how many times Richard sets up a new angle, or adjusts his lens, or asks them to change their sitting positions slightly. We're a bit of a novelty for them, an amusing enough disruption of the usual routine. The grub here matters less than the chance to get out for an hour or so and socialize, to enjoy some public life at bargain prices, watch the activities in the street market. We say our farewells.

'Well, it's been a real eye-opener,' says Albert.

THE GRAIN SHOP

'VEGETARIAN WHOLEFOOD TAKEAWAY'
PORTOBELLO ROAD

Outside the store a tall, slender young black man with discreet dreadlocks is about to tuck into his overflowing plastic container of healthy fare; his girlfriend, Claire, eats hers inside their car. He introduces himself as Chris Toussaint, a surname which prompts us into a long digression on the career of Toussaint L'Overture, a revolutionary general (much admired by the young Wordsworth), and he tells us his family came to Britain from Granada. Chris used to nurse ambitions for a career in football, and trained for a while with the Barnet team, but now his hopes lie with music: management, recording, performing. He has adopted the stage name 'Mr Redz' ('with a Z!') and says that he'll soon be releasing a CD entitled *Flavas of Mr Redz*, 'or maybe *Moods of Mr Redz*'. (The lead single will be called 'Bashment Girl' — 'that's a type of music'.) His production / management company is called '1nce in a Lifetime Ent.' — 'that's spelled with a 1, not a "once"'. Who knows, maybe he'll already be famous by the time this is published.

He favours The Grain Shop because he turned strictly vegetarian five years ago. There's not been so much as a scrap of meat in his fridge ever since. He's aware of the political and moral arguments about not eating meat, but for him the main principle was personal health. 'What do human beings get from meat?

Protein! Well, you can get protein from nuts . . . You have to ask yourself, are human beings meant to be herbivores or carnivores? My health has really improved since I turned vegetarian, I have a lot more energy.'

Our conversation is interrupted by happenstance, in the form of an unexpected passer-by, the maverick film director Richard Stanley (*Hardware, Dust Devil*), with whom I need to speak quite urgently about a documentary on Haitian Voodoo he's recently made. Richard Heeps sets up an elaborate photo session with Chris and Claire while Mr Stanley and I briefly share our admiration of the American film-maker and Voodoo priestess Maya Deren. By the time we've finished swapping contact details, two rather distinguished middle-aged West Indian men — one in a conservative grey suit, one in a bright African-style shirt and matching toque — step in and demand to know what we're up to. I explain, as best I can. The man in the African shirt ponders for a while, then asks: 'So you support Mr Blair's stand on obesity?'

Well . . . I could certainly stand to lose a few stones myself. He laughs at this. And then he launches into an extended diatribe on the current parlous state of New Labour, ending with a heartfelt lament for the untimely passing of John Smith. We all shake hands — I am jokingly (?) accused of being a Freemason — and they bestow their blessing on our trip, provided we try to 'tell the truth'.

'And you must go to Southall!'
We will, we will.

→

Flesh renounced again at **The Shahenshah**, *p.131*

Irresponsible diet advice in **Pret diet**, *p.43*

SUBWAY
BERWICK STREET MARKET, SOHO

Despite the climate of obesity scares, Subway — the chain which sells the long sandwiches that used to be known by various different names across the United States, from 'grinders' to 'subs' to 'hoagies' and 'heroes' — remains the only one of the American majors to flog its product mainly on the promise of healthy, sensible eating rather than 'fun', convenience, cheapness or Ronald McDonald. In the USA, they have built a series of television ads around the allegedly true story of a young man called Jared who lost a load of weight by calculating the calorie value of the more veggie- and salad- based Subway products, and then feeding exclusively on them for months and months. The diet worked, and the man now has a (presumably) lucrative job as walking proof of the Subway Way. His gimmick is to wave around the tent-sized pair of jeans he wore at his maximum weight. (The story is now so much a part of American pop culture that it

recently provided a storyline for the soft-centred comedy-drama series *Ed*.)

American Subway advertising also targets its primary competition, McDonald's, with an aggressive directness that is still quite rare in British advertising. The TV screen fills with what appears to be a straightforward plug for a Big Mac Meal, complete with sweet jingly music, until a scare graphic is slapped across it: this product contains 50 grams of fat!!! Cut to a luscious, meaty Subway treat which, it boasts, contains only 6 grams!!! And so on.

Subway doesn't receive much press attention, and certainly nothing like the opprobrium directed at McDonald's, and yet with some 15,000 branches in operation and about 1000 more opening every year, it is not only the second most widespread of the fast food chains but the only one that might seriously hope to challenge the McHegemony one day.

Eric Schlosser makes a number of cautionary observations about Subway in *Fast Food Nation*, though he concentrates more on the hard time the company gives its franchisees than the quality of its sandwiches. He cites one economist, who called Subway the 'worst' franchise company in America. On the plus side, the health side, Subway was the only major chain not to fall into the marketing war of constantly upping the size of its portions.

The Subway slogan: 'Choose Well'. Richard and I like the juxtaposition of the Subway entrance with the old-fashioned market stall just outside its front door, selling fresh fruit and vegetables: healthy food the old, unpackaged style versus a calculated image of healthy eating; the market versus marketing.

→

Another round of sarnies at Pret, p.39

28

FISH AND CHIPS
BERWICK STREET, SOHO

A classic fifties-style exterior, perfect for shooting from the street. Just as well, since the proprietor won't let us shoot the interior. 'Too busy, mate,' he says, nodding inside. There are just two customers.

$\rightarrow$

*Unsatisfied? Try **Burned-Out**, p.52*

PICCADILLY CIRCUS
CUSTOMERS AND WORKERS FROM PIZZA HUT,
MCDONALD'S, KFC. . .

More reticence. When the sign-holders for Pizza Hut notice Richard's camera, they hide their faces. This is baffling: they surely can't all be illegal immigrants? Dole fiddlers? Most of them look like moonlighting students, with their noses stuck into books or magazines. Still, we don't want to rain on anyone's parade, so we move on.

The crowd of lunchers on Eros are also playing shy today, especially the ladies in Islamic headscarves. And yet there are other times in our wanderings when people crave the chance to be photographed, and will do almost anything to please Richard. A few minutes later, and we've found some rather more willing victims.

→

Further McTitillation in **Outside McDonald's***, p.55*

More McCultural Criticism on p.98

LEICESTER SQUARE (1)
AND MCDONALD'S

Here's a wholesome family group who could have been posed on this bench for the occasion by a McD publicity department. Basking quietly in the sunshine, Mother and Father have their McDonald's coffees, the boys have their McFlurries. (This is the major summer promotion. The ads for it are everywhere, and all but inescapable on the London Underground. One of them features a disembodied set of achingly red female lips, floating in mid-air and parted in ecstasy as a white creamy vortex gushes into them. Outrageous.) The family look contented, and are certainly more than content to pose for us. They come from East Kilbride.

'What's your name?'

'McDonald!' says the father.

'Really?'

He laughs. 'No, it's McLean, really. We're on holiday.'

'If only you'd seen us yesterday, at All Bar One,' says the mother. 'I had a black cocktail dress on, and make-up . . .'

Just a week ago, she adds, they were eating their Big Macs on the Champs Elysées.

'We usually go to McDonald's wherever we are — you know, it's not really for us, but the boys like it.'

Was there any regional difference in the McProduct? Not that she'd noticed, but 'in France you can have a beer.'

It takes me a second or two to realize that she has launched into the famous John Travolta/Samuel L. Jackson fast-food-in-Europe routine from *Pulp Fiction*, and has the dialogue down almost word-perfect.

Jeez, everybody's an ironist these days. But, however much some global tourists dispute the point, (reasonably) impartial judgement does confirm claims that the standard McDonald product tastes exactly the same everywhere in the world. See Thomas L. Friedman, '14 Big Macs Later . . .', *New York Times*, 31 December 1995.

AN UNEXPECTED NOTE ON WARFARE

Mr Friedman, a noted political commentator, is also the author of the so-called 'Golden Arches Theory of Conflict Prevention', a proposition he first floated in a *NYT* column about a year later, in December 1996, and then expanded a little for his book, *The Lexus and the Olive Tree* (2000). Baldly stated, it is Friedman's contention that 'no two countries that both have a McDonald's have ever fought a war against each other'. Cute, but, as other observers have pointed out, it depends how you define 'war'. India (McDonald's turf since 1996) and Pakistan (since 1998) have certainly shed plenty of their armed forces' blood over control of the Kargil heights.

LEICESTER SQUARE (2)
AND KFC

Hungry from his labours, Richard needs lunch and opts for KFC, his favourite takeaway. I inform him that, in my distant youth, this product was held in such low esteem by me and my peers that we used to call it Kentucky Fried Chuckup.

Richard is reluctant to defend his choice on any grounds other than the *non est disputandum* one that, in common with millions of others, he likes the taste. I suppose that if I felt like playing Devil's Advocate for the fowl friers I could supply him with at least one smart rejoinder, by pointing out that the KFC is the only major McWorld product to retain at some touch with the realm of traditional meat consumption — simply, by retaining bones.

One commentator (Mennell, 1985, p.349) has suggested that the triumph of the American burger in its homeland may well owe much to the fact that its smashed-up meat products have nothing unpleasantly reminiscent of the living, breathing, mooing cow. By 1979, 40 per cent of all American beef was being consumed in this sanitized form. Today? Americans are notoriously more squeamish than the British when it comes to what we call offal and they call 'variety meats' or 'organ meats', just as we tend to be far more squeamish about those succulent and nutritious innards than the French, the Italians and the Spanish.

Instead, I try to shame and disgust Richard about his KFC habit by reading a horror story from this morning's *Independent*, which reports that animal rights activists in the United States have made a clandestine video which shows bored workers at a KFC factory subjecting chickens to all manner of outlandish tortures: spitting tobacco juice into their eyes, stamping on them, hurling them at walls . . .

'Yeah, but that's America, isn't it?' he says, and carries on munching cheerily.

→

*More fowl play at **The Garden Chinese** on p.56*

DIXIE CHICKS

Most people know at least a bit about the KFC epic, but here it is in miniature: 'Colonel' Harlan Sanders (1890–1980), who founded the chain in 1952, was about as much a real colonel as 'Duke' Ellington was a British Peer of the Realm. His 'title', bestowed in 1935, came from an outfit called the Honorable Order of Kentucky Colonels. A lifelong hustler, mountebank, charlatan and loser, he had practised law without a law degree, obstetrics without a medical degree, and achieved a spectacular lack of success in many other fields of endeavour.

His first real breakthrough came quite late in life, when he opened a popular restaurant. Though he was obliged to sell this business to pay off debts, he drew on the experience by going from town to town peddling his 'secret recipe' for chicken flavouring to other restaurateurs. Consisting of eleven herbs and spices, the recipe had, he said, been perfected by him when he was working at a Kentucky service station in the 1930s. It was in the early 1950s that he adopted the full Southern Colonel persona, complete with white suit and string tie, by way of cheap and effective publicity. Sanders opened the first KFC in Salt Lake City, and within a decade the concern had grown into the largest restaurant chain of its day, with some 600 units. It was eventually bought by Pepsi in 1964, for $2 million, and is now owned by Tricon Global Restaurants, who also own Pizza Hut and Taco Bell. Sanders eventually became a born-again Christian, but could never quite shed his vice of swearing.

When Richard is sated, we throw the bones and other remnants on the grass for the pigeons. Richard photographs the quasi-cannibalistic feeding frenzy. It looks great from my point of view, very dramatic, but Richard suspects that it reads a lot better to the naked eye than the camera. What's more, he's nagged by the memory that Martin Parr (whose trademark deadpan, sardonic style, we have agreed, is to be regarded as the antithesis of what we are after in our present assignment) may have done a version of this shot. We wander over to a photographic bookshop in Charing Cross Road to check out a couple of Parr's recent books. Answer: not quite, though there is a shot which juxtaposes a pigeon and some KFC litter.

'Your shot is much more intense,' I assure him, and resist the temptation to mention Bataille, or Nietzsche's aphorism that there is no feast without cruelty. But I suspect that the pigeons won't make it into print.

FISH

COD	
ROCK SALMON	355
PLAICE	355
SCAMPI	355
HADDOCK	395
SKATE	475
CHIPS	495
	SML 100 LRG 200

PIES & SAUSAGES

STEAK & KIDNEY	
CHICKEN & MUSHROOM	170
BEEF & ONION	170
CORNISH PASTY	170
SAUSAGE	170
SAVELOY	100
	100

GRILLED

CHICKEN SHISH
CHICKEN FILLET BURGER

FRIED C

1 PC
2 PCS
3 PCS
4 PCS
MEGA BOX
8 PCS CHICKEN, 4 CHIPS & BOTTLE D

"Hot & Tasty" Chicken just the way you like it!

TAKE AV

TAKE A

LEICESTER SQUARE: AN HISTORICAL ODDITY

Perhaps the strangest single outlet in the history of London's fast food experience was a street lamp, erected here in 1898. For the price of a halfpenny, a spout on the lower part of the lamp would disgorge a quart of hot water. Another part of the structure provided coffee, cocoa, and tablets of beef-tea concentrate. The novelty was a great success, so much so that the crowds which gathered round it were declared a public nuisance, and the dispenser was torn down within a year.

→

More liquid refreshment at **Nin Com Soup**, *p.85*

PRET A MANGER
BATEMAN STREET, SOHO

Whatever your view of its tastiness, hipness or value for money, there can be little doubt as to which British chain outlet has the most consistently pleasing design scheme, both inside and out. Richard is particularly thrilled by Pret A Manger's chrome floors, but he also waxes enthusiastic about the well-lit open metal cabinets, the high stools, the distinctive lettering and the red and white star logo. The clean, crisply articulated lines of the PAM 'Comments' box render him almost speechless with excitement. I suggest that he enjoy himself for a while, giving me the chance to ruminate.

→
*Revisit the BLT at **Tooting Broadway**, p.91*

CONFESSIONS OF A PRET CONNOISSEUR

I have been dipping into a recommended volume about the sociology of food choice — enough to ruin anyone's appetite — and tried in vain to find anything of so much as passing interest there. One of the few extractable lessons, perhaps, is that people tend to lie about their food choices, and about the reasons for their food choices. A fully paid anthropologist might have the time and energy to note in detail the discrepancies between avowed and actual purchases, but the quickest means of tackling the fantasy factor is the time-honoured one of honest introspection.

I thus decide that it is about time to do the decent, post-Malinowskian participant-observer thing by casting an introspective gaze over my own habitual patterns of fast food consumption, and asking what role fantasies or half-admitted associations of ideas has played in the whole strange business of building my brand loyalty. For Pret A

Manger, I realize, has come to play an uncomfortably large part in said patterns. One reason for the sense of discomfort here is my awareness that in 2001 McDonald's bought 33 per cent of the Pret A Manger chain, so that my purchases are contributing directly to the coffers of the Evil Empire. A personal boycott may be the only ethical way forward.

This needs thought. When I am working on a long-term writing or research project, I stay pretty much at home all day, cook for myself and hardly touch fast food for weeks at a stretch. But when I am nipping around on assorted hackish tasks, then a vast chunk of my sustenance in daylight hours is derived from two main outlets: Upper Crust at railway stations, Pret A Manger in (mainly London) town. (Note: the term 'upper crust', meaning posh, is said to be derived from the medieval practice of cooking mass quantities of bread in large ovens. The poor took the bread from the lower part, which was charred by its closeness to the coals, and thus partly spoiled. The upper crust went to the upper crust.)

So what dreams and realities have I been buying from Pret over the past decade?

A I flirted for a while with the Turkey and Cranberry Salad sandwich. Mixed and wholly contradictory reveries of health and feasting hover around this selection: on the left brain (logic), turkey is well known to have one of the lowest fat contents of all meats; on the right brain (intuition and emotion), I reminisce fondly about those early eighties Thanksgiving dinners in Alabama and

→

Another helping of turkey at **The Vaults**, *p.135*

41

Tennessee. Choice soon dropped, because the meat is too bland and the cranberry sauce much, much too sweet.

B Tuna mayo sandwich. Virtuous choice, soothing to one's inner Puritan. A solid, fairly-priced hit of good quality fishy protein; will keep you going happily for at least three hours; no furry creatures with liquid brown eyes killed in the making. But, frankly, just a bit on the boring side — like many Brits, I prefer my tuna mayo adulterated with, for example, some chewy bits of sweetcorn. (Tuna and sweetcorn is the main 'regional variant' of the United Kingdom as an optional topping in Domino's Pizza. In Japan the variants include squid; in France, crème fraiche; in India, lamb and pickled ginger; in Guatemala, black bean sauce.) Choice largely dropped.

C Crayfish and (I think) rocket sandwich. Sounds tangy and succulent and interestingly hybrid, no? Huck Finn on the Mississippi meets Jean de Florette in his herb garden. As with prawns, though, crayfish can sometimes trigger some atavistic tingle of disgust, the notion that spidery things with exoskeletons are not a true part of my tribal food. Choice dropped.

D Sushi box. Allegedly healthy and slimming, conspicuously 'sophisticated' and twenty-first century. (My parents still shudder at the mere mention of raw fish.) In my less than expert view, PAM branches do a damn good box of mixed sushi goodies, but it certainly isn't cheap (more than a fiver for the carnivore kind, and who honestly wants the vegetarian?) and — like all sushi — it does not fill my large and demanding occidental belly unless wolfed down on the kind of scale which makes my bank manager weep salt tears. An occasional indulgence.

So in the end, I nearly always come back to one of three classics, all admirably filling and more than adequately tasty:

Club sandwich, BLT, and/or Egg and Tomato on Rye, a wonderfully harmonious yet strangely unpredictable blend of flavours and textures which takes a lot of beating around, say, 11a.m. Perfect brunch food.

If I eat in the store (infrequent, mainly because I resent the swingeing VAT mark-up), I take the opportunity to read the complimentary copy of a certain bilious tabloid which has made its fortune from terrifying the wives of Middle England — you know the one. Over time, this bad habit will no doubt have the Pavlovian effect of making me taste bacon every time I hear the phrase 'asylum seeker'. If not, I inhale the food at an unhealthily fast rate while walking to my next appointment, bin the wrappings as soon as possible (I grew up in the pre-littering generation) and go about my largely undemanding chores with the comforting sensation that my innards will be calmed for most of the working day.

At one time, when I wanted to lose weight in a hurry, I went for a couple of weeks on a diet of no more than two PAM mayo-free chicken salad sandwiches *per diem*, plus all the coffee (no sugar) and water I felt like drinking. I recommend this restricted diet to absolutely nobody, least of all the litigious, and I can't say that those were the most pleasant weeks of my life, but it worked for me. I may do it again, when this short book is written.

$\rightarrow$

More raw fish at **Sushi Noto**, p.112

44

A NOTE ON SANDWICH BARS

According to the scholarly Antony Clayton, the country's earliest sandwich chain was opened in 1918 by Kenelm Foss, who enjoyed some notoriety as an actor, author and film director. (See also E. Hooten-Smith, *The Restaurants of London*, 1928.) It was called Sandy's All-British Sandwich Bar, and the first branch was in Oxenden Street. 'No shell-fish; no tinned food; no foreign produce; no tips; no waiting', its sign bragged, to the confusion of those of us today who consider shellfish a pricey luxury. Sandy's offered no fewer than sixty types of sandwich, priced from 4d to 6d, and its specials included 'King Edward's Favourite' (Stilton, celery and parsley) and a toasted treat with the now-unthinkable name of 'The Swastika' (grilled ham, egg and tomato, with double Gloucester cheese and sherry sauce.) Memories of the 'Germans' episode of *Fawlty Towers* — So let's see: that's two Swastikas, one Panzer, a Blitzkrieg and two double Himmlers . . .

HOT DOG STAND

OPPOSITE THE HOUSES OF PARLIAMENT,
WESTMINSTER

Trade is thriving near the Gothic Revival skirts
of the Mother of Parliaments, although — since
the temperature is well up into the seventies
today — more in cold, fizzy drinks and ice cream
than in hot dogs. There is a pancake shack here,
too, where you can munch your freshly made
apricot crêpe while admiring the view across to
the London Eye; and a stand flogging assorted
tourist tat, in which representations of Great
Englishmen such as Sherlock Holmes and Jack
the Ripper play a large part.

*Wurst to come at **Hot Dog Stand**,
p.57*

ON HOT DOGS
AND THE ENGLISH
HOT DOG

According to Jeffrey Steingarten in *It Must've Been Something I Ate*, the modern hot dog was invented by a Jewish-Bavarian sausage vendor by the name of Anton (some sources give Antoine) Feuchtwanger, who had a stall at the St Louis Exposition of 1903. At first, he would lend his customers white gloves so that they could keep their fingers clean while they ate his franks, but people would just keep walking off with them. He turned for help to his brother, a baker, and the hot dog roll was born. The name, or more exactly the term 'hot dog' (meaning, roughly, 'oh boy!' or 'wow!') had already been in existence for several years (*OED* gives 1896 as its earliest use) and the exclamation soon found itself fastened to the weenie in a bun.

Steingarten concedes that there are other versions of this story. The acerbic American wit, H.L. Mencken, ascribes the invention of the hot dog to one Harry Mozley Stevens, caterer at the New York Polo Grounds, and dates it to 1905, but a closer examination of the Mencken account shows that Stevens's only real innovations were warming the hot dog buns and adding various condiments.

The American hot dog has inspired a respectable body of literature from Mencken onwards, of which one of the high points is John Kennedy Toole's *A Confederacy of Dunces*. The hero of Toole's novel, a grossly proportioned and misanthropic medievalist called Ignatius J. Reilley, finds brief but colourful employment as a vendor of 'weenies' (he winds up consuming most of them himself, with catastrophic effects on his digestion). I recommend the book heartily.

The English hot dog, a keenly anticipated favourite of my childhood, seems to have been somewhat marginalized in recent years, and today tends to be served not so much in chain restaurants as by dodgy geezers in dodgy vans outside sporting events. (But the football chant aimed at supposedly overweight players, like Gazza, is 'Who ate all the pies? Who ate all the pies? You fat bastard, you fat bastard, you ate all the pies!') Often, the UK hot dog's meat component will not be a frankfurter, but a classic English banger or snorker. And where Americans usually confine themselves to ketchup and mustard dressing, with sauerkraut an occasional fancy extra, the British palate calls for lots and lots of sloppy fried onions.

Notwithstanding our penchant for hot, spicy foods, the United Kingdom has proved largely resistant to that aggressive mutant form of the hot dog, the chilli dog. (Similarly, I doubt there is one British citizen in ten who could tell you much about sloppy joes.)

ON KETCHUP

Once again, I am indebted to the assiduous food critic of *Vogue*, Mr Steingarten, though this time to an essay, 'Playing Ketchup', in his earlier volume, *The Man Who Ate Everything*. The indefatigable Steingarten taste-tested 35 different brands of ketchup, using ten large orders of McDonald's French fries as the blotter. Regular old Heinz 57 came out pretty much top of the heap ('Bright color, thick but a bit sticky, quite sweet; less taste than home-made but with a good, fruity acidity, some tomato taste: unassertive and uninteresting spices. With French fries, a marriage made in heaven . . . .'), with serious competition being offered only by A&P Tomato Ketchup, Del Monte and Hunt's.

The Heinz brand, incidentally, has remained more or less identical since it was launched in America's bicentennial year, 1876, at the Philadelphia World's Fair. By 1896, according to the *New York Tribune*, ketchup had become America's national condiment. Today, the Heinz brand holds 55 per cent of the US ketchup market, with Hunt's at 19 per cent and Del Monte at 7 per cent. Steingarten's work also established two other key pieces of ketchupiana.

A Londoners can take pride in the fact that the modern form of ketchup was first invented in our own dear town. The recipe appeared in Alexander Hunter's *Culina Famulatric Medicinae; or, Receipts in Cookery*, published in 1804 (and thereby significantly antedated the better-known recipe published in Maria Rundell's *A New System of Domestic Cookery*, 1813, which is filched unacknowledged from Hunter anyway). Keen cooks may care to try it:

'Take tomatas [sic] when ripe, and bake them in an oven, till they become perfectly soft, then scoop them out with a tea-spoon, and rub the pulp through a sieve. To the pulp, put as much chilli vinegar as will bring it to proper thickness, with salt to the taste. Add to each quart, half an ounce of garlic and one ounce of shallot, both sliced very thin. Boil during the space of a quarter of an hour, taking care to skim the mixture very well. Then strain, and take out the garlic and shallot . . . and let it stand for a few days before it is corked up.'

B The name — and 'ketchup', 'catsup' and 'catchup' are three variant words for just the one substance — appears to have antedated the thing, or so it would appear if you trace the origins of the modern term back to *koe-chiap* or *ke-tsiap* in a Chinese dialect known as Amoy (where it meant the brine of pickled fish), or to the Malaysian *ketchap*, itself possibly a Chinese import word meaning a kind of sweet soy sauce. 'Catsup' first crops up as an English word in 1690; 'ketchup' in 1711. I recall an episode of *The Simpsons* in which the evil multi-millionaire Mr Burns, suddenly rendered a pauper, has to shop in a supermarket for the first time in his life. Faced with a bewildering choice between 'catsup' and 'ketchup', he lapses into despair.

BURNED-OUT FISH AND CHIP SHOP
NEAR KING'S CROSS

A sort of multivalent fast food *memento mori*, a reminder not just that business for the independent restaurant can be precarious in the extreme, but also that the once-ubiquitous fish and chip shop has been forced back into the Second Division of British fast food.

Fish and chips, like bacon and eggs, now seems such an inevitable combination — Churchill, it seems, borrowed a phrase from J.B. Priestley and called them 'The Good Companions' — and the dish itself so deeply entrenched a part of British experience that it comes as a mild shock to discover how recently those edible companions palled up. The immediate antecedent of fish'n'chips was the street snack of fried fish, served cold in bread — Dickens, in *Oliver Twist* (1839), refers to a 'fried fish warehouse'. In 1851, Henry Mayhew noted the prevalence of cold, fried fish on a piece of bread as a pub snack, and estimated that there were some 300 street sellers of fried fish (as against another 300-odd selling pea soup and hot eels, with about 150 selling whelks). Four years later, in 1855, Watts Phillips's *The Wild Tribes of London* describes a Jewish-owned fried fish shop, selling hot fish to a mainly Jewish clientele, but makes no mention of spuds.

So the earliest appearance of the Great British Chip in literature appears to be in *A Tale of Two Cities*, published in 1859, in which Dickens mentions 'husky chips of potatoes, fried with some reluctant drops of oil'. And chips finally met their match in London some time around 1860 — at any rate, Mr Joseph Main of Cleveland Street later claimed to have been in the fish and chip trade since 1860; his claim was challenged by a Mr Lees of Mossley, near Oldham, who appears to have sold fish and chips from a wooden hut in the town market from *c*.1863.

Within a couple of decades, fish and chips was established as the staple proletarian foodstuff it would remain for most of the early twentieth century. George Gissing, in *Workers in the Dawn* (1880), describes a fried fish shop in Whitecross Street that sounds almost exactly like the standard modern version:

. . . behind the long counter stands a man and a woman, the former busy in frying flat fish over a huge fire, the latter engaged in dipping a ladle into a large vessel which steams profusely; and in front of the counter stands a row of hungry looking people, eagerly devouring the flakes of fish and greasy potatoes as they come from the pan, while others are served by the woman to little basins of stewed eels from the steaming tureen.

By 1914, there were an estimated 25,000 fish and chip shops in Britain.

→

For a highly recommended one, see The Fishcotheque, p.93

AT YOUR CONVENIENCE

Browsing through the literature of fish'n'chips introduces me to the relatively unsung figure of Raymond Postgate (1896–1971), a man who did more than almost any single agitator to raise the level of British eating in the twentieth century. The brother-in-law of, and occasional collaborator with, the eminent socialist historian G.D.H. Cole, Postgate was an interesting, multifaceted man — a conscientious objector in the First World War, a founder member of the Communist Party of Great Britain, an editor of *Tribune* and a civil servant with the Board of Trade — who had none of the British Socialist's traditional lack of interest in gastronomy. In fact, it was Postgate who founded the *Good Food Guide* in 1951. He published each of the next ten issues or so from his own house, finally handing the enterprise over to the Consumers' Association in 1962. Something of a wit, Postgate famously observed of the term 'convenience food' that 'the adjective, with its lavatorial connotations, is well-chosen'. He alliteratively characterized most London restaurant offerings as 'sodden, sour, slimy, sloppy, stale or saccharined', and once proposed founding a Society for the Prevention of Cruelty to Food.

Think of him the next time your sandwich strikes you as quite nice, really.

54

OUTSIDE McDONALD'S
NEAR PICCADILLY CIRCUS

ICE CREAM VAN
HAYMARKET

Richard lines up a photograph of another version of the McFlurry advert. As blatantly erotic as the Pop Art version of lips and creamy vortex that we've been encountering on the Underground, this consists primarily of a young woman pouting pinkly into camera, and the slogan 'In Your Dreams'. The pure in spirit will read this as meaning 'The McFlurry is the kind of delicious ambrosia you enjoy consuming in happy dreams'. The rest of us, if so inclined by our sexuality, remain fixated on the woman's challenging-inviting lips. In our dreams . . .

Less dubious commentary on
McDonald's *on p.98*

More desserts at ***Raghuvanshi***
Sweets*, p.126*

Richard, always fascinated by the Populuxe style of 1950s and 1960s Americana, is drawn to the van's rich nursery pinks and blues like a bear to a honeypot. Most Londoners are, one suspects, still dimly aware that the sale of ice cream in Britain owes something to immigrants from Italy. Far fewer know much about the key players in this story, such as Carlo Gatti, who was one of the most powerful figures in the Victorian catering industry, arrived in London all but penniless, and made his first living from a coffee stall which also sold *goffre*, small, sugary waffles. In 1849 he joined forces with another Italian immigrant, one Signor Bolla, and opened an ice cream shop at 129 Holborn Hill. In the first volume of *London Labour and the London Poor*, Mayhew noted: '. . . the sale of ice creams was unknown in the streets until last summer, and was first introduced, as a matter of speculation, by a man who was acquainted with the confectionery business, and who purchased his ices from a confectioner in Holborn.'

In the 1860s, hundreds of Italians were driven into political exile; many of them chose Britain as their new home. By 1881, the Italian population of London was estimated at about 3500, and had all but monopolized the street ice cream trade. The product was sold in small conical glasses, known as 'licks', and the standard portion was a 'penny lick'. Browsers in late Victorian literature will come across references to the 'hokey-pokey man', so called because Italian vendors would try to attract customers by handing out small samples saying '*Ecco un poco*' ('here's a little bit'). By 1900, there were some 900 ice cream barrows on the streets of London, and most of them were sent out from Clerkenwell, where rival immigrant families concocted their particular, top-secret recipes in domestic kitchens.

This all sounds rather charming and folkloric. But in Glasgow, rival Italian families have been known to fight each other viciously for control of turf — the 'ice cream wars', immortalized in Bill Douglas's underrated film *Comfort and Joy.*

THE GARDEN CHINESE
RESTAURANT AND CAFE
CHINATOWN

As noted above, re Indian restaurants, very few
Chinese eating establishments readily qualify
as fast food, particularly here in Chinatown.
(London's second Chinatown; the first was in
Limehouse, and survived until the Second World
War. Another story.) This is a terrible frustration
in visual terms, since the glistening, syrupy-
brown skins of roasted Peking duck and the
matt orangey coils of cooked squid are every
bit as tempting to the lens as to the palate. The
Garden Restaurant is one of the exceptions,
since it has an active take-away counter as well
as a dining area. They welcome us in, provided
we do not hamper trade. Richard shoots and
shoots, photographically hungry for these distinctive shades and textures.

$\rightarrow$

A less tempting Chinese offering at
Chopstix*, p.96*

HOT DOG STAND
OUTSIDE THE BRITISH MUSEUM

The vendor himself refuses to be photographed, but his product — which, as we expected, features a long, plump English snorker, not an American-style frankfurter — cries out for good, saturated colour stock, particularly when slathered in interweaving strands of shiny red ketchup and gleaming yellow mustard.

His customers are as multi-cultural as you would hope from this major tourist resort. Among the contented chompers are a trio of young Korean girls, a complementary trio of young Japanese girls, a one-child nuclear family from Beijing. (Chinese government birth control regulations, strictly one child per couple, have created a new generation of highly indulged, only children, sometimes called 'Little Emperors' and 'Little Empresses'. It is the — corrupted? — taste of this spoiled generation which has helped make McDonald's such a roaring triumph in China.)

'Are you a professional?' the Chinese wife asks Richard, impressed by the unfashionable rectangular bulk of his camera.

'Definitely,' Richard replies, showing her the word 'Professional' written on its body.

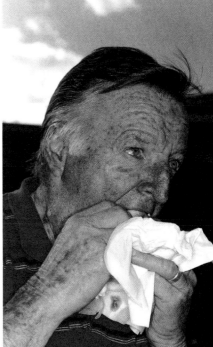

After a while, we fall into discussion with Mike and John, two chaps from Australia, late sixties or thereabouts, 'and we're bloody hungry!' Mike, who emigrated from Croydon in 1966, takes a mild professional interest in mass-produced food, since he 'used to be second cook on a tanker. Mind you, all that meant was emptying out the garbage and peeling the bloody spuds!' He and his pal make it back to the UK about once every ten years, on average, but 'I don't think we'll be coming again.' Oh, come on now, I say, in what is meant to be an encouraging tone, assuming that he means that he'll probably be dead by 2014. But what he means is that he can't stand the overcrowding in London. He hates the masses.

→
Mysteries of the saveloy revealed in
On the Saveloy, *p.94*

BURGER KING
TOTTENHAM COURT ROAD

This chain's big tie-in movie of the month is *Spider-Man 2*, directed by the fitfully interesting Sam Raimi (who began his career back in the 1980s with *The Evil Dead*) and reputedly not such a bad effort, as summer blockbusters go. Images of the neurotic teenage superhero are everywhere, and the kitchen is turning out 'web fries' for the really keen *Spider* fan.

Burger King seems not to arouse nearly so much curiosity (love, loyalty, contempt, rage) as McDonald's, and I suspect that most of its customers couldn't care less about its whys and hows. The chain began life round about the same time as McDonald's did, as the Insta-Burger-King restaurants of Southern California. Its subsequent development would make for an interesting study in commercial Darwinism: it survived and flourished where dozens, if not hundreds, of apparently identical competitors went to the wall.

The triumph undoubtedly owes much to the revolutionary duo, Dave Edgerton and Jim McLamore, both of whom held degrees from Cornell, a positively stratospheric level of qualification amongst the generation of fast food pioneers, almost none of whom had made it past high school. Insta-Burger-King, like McDonald's, had begun to develop a franchise system, but it wasn't doing at all well at the time (1954) when Edgerton bought an IBK franchise for Dade County, Miami, Florida.

He succeeded by using scorched-earth methods, threw out the Insta-Burger-King instruction book, radically re-designed the standard-issue broiler (said to have been what the Americans call a Rube Goldberg and the British a Heath Robinson contraption), and made a huge hit with the public by coming up with BK's answer to the neutron bomb: a quarter-pound hamburger, the Whopper. By 1957, Edgerton and McLamore had rebranded their business as 'Burger King, Home of the Whopper', and within a few years had bought out the national rights to the parent chain. By 1967, Burger King's expansion programme had passed the hundred new restaurants per year mark, finally equal to McDonald's. In the same year, BK was acquired by the Pillsbury Corporation, then the third-largest packaged foods company in the United States. By 1985, the average McDonald's outlet generated sales of $1.3 million per annum, but BK was not so very far behind, with average sales of $1.09 million.

Just thought you might like to know.

$\rightarrow$

The best burger in town? See
Bubba's, p.68

RAY THE POET
BURGER KING
KING'S CROSS STATION

Ray's product loyalty to the Home of the Whopper is unwavering. He's willing, at a pinch, to tolerate a McDonald's milkshake, but when it comes to burgers, it has to be a BK cheeseburger meal deal (£4.99) every time. He cradles the three basic components — burger, fries, large fizzy drink — like a nursing mother with her baby, and soon demolishes the lot.

Ray, who's about fifty and lives on a housing estate in South London with his brother and widowed mother, is a very interesting man, though you might not guess quite how interesting from his CV. He's unemployed at the moment, has been for several years now, and has had more than his fair share of unemployment and protracted illness over the last three decades. He broke up with his long-term girlfriend a couple of years ago. But where so many others trapped on benefit tend to lapse into apathy and inertia, Ray — who in the 1980s took a degree in philosophy as a mature student — has become a ferocious autodidact, following course after course after course at the special low rate for people on benefit. You name it, there's a fair chance he's studied it: stained-glass-making, jewellery-making, sculpture (abstract), film history, art history, German for Conversation . . . and, most important, Creative Writing. Ray has many intellectual passions — above all for military history (in happier days, he belonged to war-gaming groups, and what he doesn't know about the Punic Wars ain't worth knowing) — but Creative Writing has become central to his life.

He has lots of ideas for novels, he says, though he finds it hard to sit down and carry out the plots that he's planned. But he feels no such block when it comes to poetry, which he writes down furiously into a small, black note-book, and will read out on request even to near-strangers. It's confessional poetry, almost wholly about his darkest thoughts; suicidal thoughts, at times. He takes it along to a group he belongs to these days, Survivor's Poetry, and sometimes he reads it out, when the mood is right: too often, he says, the meetings are dominated by people who behave as though they're at a competitive poetry slam, and shout or declaim their works, drowning out all the shy and introspective types who might just benefit from a few minutes at the centre of attention.

On the whole, Ray shuns fast food as unhealthy and eats with his family at home. It's usually just on nights when he's hurrying to his poetry meetings that he stops off for a quick refuel at BK. Richard is fascinated by the ambiguous quality of Ray's appearance: 'He could be a businessman, he could be an intellectual, he could be a tramp.' Ray hears this, and likes what he hears.

'I've been all three,' he says.

PERFECT FRIED CHICKEN
STOKE NEWINGTON

We are trying to set up some other shots, but a pouting mixed-race Lolita called Charlie, sitting athwart a fancy bicycle, keeps demanding that Richard take her picture. We have been wary throughout of photographing children and teenagers without permission, but this is such a public solicitation that there seems no harm in it, so Richard shoots away.

Fifteen minutes later, a belligerent-looking boy who can't be more than a year older than Charlie comes barrelling into the shop and demands a percentage of the fee we owe 'my woman'. He doesn't seem to be kidding, but I call his bluff anyway. Of course, I say, 40 per cent all right? And he guffaws: he's a nice kid, really, not a hard case at all, and was just mucking us around.

A quartet of thick-set Polish men have been watching us, and we ask if they'd mind posing, too. They would mind it very much, it seems. But Poland is in the EU now: this can't be a visa scam?

→ _____
Sitting down with chickens at
Nando's, p.65

CHICKEN VILLAGE PIZZA
STOKE NEWINGTON

Three skinny Asian boys, teenage or thereabouts, gangle in the street, long strings of mozzarella dangling from their mouths to their pizza slices like lengths of chewing gum. A timid pensioner might well find them threatening, and my guess is that they would really quite like to be taken for Well 'Ard . . . which probably means that they are anything but. Sure enough, Saj turns out to have a highly respectable job at the Halifax, just down the road, and his two pals Ayud and Zafar, are both students. Saj has the gift of the gab, but his friends are as shy as can be, and find it hard to speak to us much above whispers. Moral: you CAN still judge by appearances, provided you remember that the codes are a bit more complicated than they were.

CITY KEBAB HOUSE
STOKE NEWINGTON

The place is deserted, but a poster, so horrible that it fascinates, dominates the counter and the window space: NATIONAL KEBAB WEEK 2004, it proclaims — some promotional nonsense dreamed up by an alcopop company (they didn't pay me, I won't name them). The poster shows an English Everyberk, bald and grinning, holding his pop in one hand and an obscene organic shape only faintly resembling a kebab — distended by Photoshop, Richard thinks — in the other. Lurid, ketchupy lettering spells out the message: GO ON! STUFF YOUR FACE! Thank you, but I have other plans.

→

*Crusader kebabs in **Medieval kebab**, p.83*

LEICESTER SQUARE
REVISITED

At dusk, the place is a lot more melancholic than at lunchtime; mildly unpleasant, too, thanks to a disgusting smell which keeps wafting in our direction. Malfunctioning sewers? Stagnant water in the fountain? A mildly barmy Nigerian woman accosts me as though I am the local sanitary inspector, and angrily demands an explanation; then cross-examines me on a variety of subjects from property prices in Manchester to the state of the railway system.

While I am thus detained, Richard snaps and snaps: Elena, a student from Hanover, sharing pizza; Ben, who's doing A levels in Travel and Tourism (those are A levels?) chomping on a Burger King; Kyla enjoying her vegetarian moussaka, which she's brought here from Food for Thought in Covent Garden ('I don't really like fast food. I like my food to be . . . made'); Kamran, a spiky-haired student of Digital Media Arts, making a meal of his Subway; taciturn Paul, grumpily demolishing his last slices of deep-pan pizza.

The West End is letting us down; time to head south.

NANDO'S
CLAPHAM HIGH STREET

Richard adores the restaurants in the Nando's chain, they're far and away his favourite place for a sit-down meal, so we stop here for a mid-evening refuel before working the neighbourhood. 'Have you ever eaten at Nando's before?' asks the waitress as you come in — a less pointless question than it seems, since Nando's operates a system halfway between fast food and conventional restaurant. You pick a table, designated with a little flag, check out your menu, head back to the counter, place your order and pay. The food appears almost disconcertingly quickly. And I have to admit, it's really OK, though not if your idea of a restaurant evening involves protracted lingering over your coffee, brandy and Havanas. We are in, fully fed and out in well under half an hour, Richard mildly disgruntled that he forgot to claim the free refills on his fizzy drink.

Clapham High Street is changed, changed utterly, since the last time I visited. Walking from Clapham North to Clapham Common Stations is like a trip upwards through the British class structure: you start with the humble, the plain and the faintly scuzzy — down-at-heel Chinese counters, deserted West Indian takeaways — and you ascend through a variety of themed bars to a sort of Yuppie Nirvana near the Common itself. There is, for instance, a gigantic deli here, lights blazing well into the evening, the shelves of which are crammed beyond the lushest dreams of gourmandizing with exotic treats, and which would put rival outfits in Notting Hill, Knightsbridge or, come to that, Milan or Manhattan to shame. Every other boozer seems to be a Cuban bar, a Brazilian bar, a Venezuelan bar, an Argentinian bar and probably a Guatemalan bar, while the restaurants tend towards the posh hybrid — crosses between a Kyoto monastery and a Florentine perfume store. Stap me vitals, this is Clapham?

But at the dowdy end of the road is 'Grandma's', a quaint little place which used to be known as 'the Hole in the Wall' and is still exactly that. From a working space not much bigger than a phone box, a pretty West Indian woman dispenses an array of dead cheap fare from her home territories. A quid gets me a Saltfish Jamaica Pattie (not bad for a microwaved product: a bit like a spicy tuna and sweetcorn sandwich, served hot, watch out for the fine bones) and a friendly if wary conversation through the tiny serving hatch. 'Grandma', it emerges, is not a mythical figure but a real old lady, who ran this business for many years until she grew a bit too feeble for the work, and passed it on; she is still alive and reasonably well. The sign outside 'Grandma's' boasts 24-hour service, but the reality is that they tend to close down not too long after midnight, when trade grows scarce. I am rather enchanted by the place, but she is justifiably suspicious of our motives and won't let Richard photograph. Pity.

It's been a long day. We need a couple of beers, and then bed.

$\rightarrow$

*Malaysian chicken at **Kota Satay**, p.68*

A1 CAFE
ROMAN ROAD, MILE END

It is raining heavily this morning, so Richard and I are sheltering here for a while, eavesdropping a little on the men eating their massive fry-ups, noting the workmen coming in from building sites for their cans of fizzy drink or plastic cups of tea. Richard takes shots of the impromptu still-life compositions offered by salt and pepper pots, mustard squeezers and ketchup bottles, while I flick through some of my research materials, which today include a Penguin *History of Food*. Since we are on the Roman Road — which I am assured really was a Roman road, two millennia ago, when the Legions policed Londinium — I am particularly keen to track down a few details of fast food under the Empire.

In Imperial Rome itself, I am by now not too surprised to learn, fast food was an essential component of proletarian life. Just as in London, until comparatively recent decades: if you were affluent enough, you would live in a fair-sized house of stone and brick and have your own fire on which to cook, or have servants cook for you. But the Roman poor lived crowded into the equivalent of blocks of flats — *insulae*, 'islands' — often mainly wooden; places in which it was far too hazardous ever to light fires. So every block or so would have a commercial cook-house, where you would either pay for your bit of meat or fish to be heated, or would buy the cooked goods on sale. Thus, Roman fast food might be defined as the food of those who did not own fire. Interesting. I make a note to tell Richard that we need some images of flames today.

Back to the present. Mr Selcuk Polat, who manages the A1 Cafe, is one of the many owners who is pleased to have our attention, and even demands to be photographed, hamming it up for the camera. To explain the sort of photography in which he specializes, Richard gives one of the waitresses a postcard showing a diner he shot in California. She looks at it with interest, and notes how it derives some of its effect from the contrast between the front and rear of the image: the foreground is a still life, the background is filled with motion. Spot on! I have known full-time photography students who wouldn't have grasped the point so quickly.

A container lorry arrives, with a mass delivery of plastic takeaway containers and Cokes. I make a note to look into the whole question of fizzy drinks.

The rain has eased. Time for other quarters of the East End.

→
*Why fizzy drinks are lethal as well as disgusting in **Killer Sugars**, p.108*

KOTA SATAY
SPITALFIELDS MARKET

If you wanted to illustrate the proposition that any form of national cuisine could potentially be marketed as fast food, you could do a lot worse than come here, where a United Nations of fast food huts is nestled under the one roof:

Falafels
Crêpes
The Potato Hut
Pacific Paradise
Tandoori Hut
The Austro-Hungarian Cafe

Not to overlook the place which sells 'Square Pies', hugely successful, my foodie friends tell me. For our lunch, Richard and I opt — no very strong reason, whim mainly — for Malaysian, at the Kota Satay. A fair-sized chuck of hot chicken on a stick, sloppy fried noodles with vegetables, a bottle of cold water. (By the 'Vivat' company, whose product seems to be cropping up everywhere on our wanderings. Perhaps, I speculate, they have a special deal with the London catering trade? The small print confirms this guess: 'Vivat' is bottled by a Fast Food Distribution Company from Enfield.) Total: £3.50. Quality: blandly acceptable. Men in business suits take late lunches at the tables near us; two of them, David and Phil, turn out to work for the property company which runs the Market.

BUBBA'S ARKANSAS CAFE PIT B-B-Q
SPITALFIELDS MARKET

This is the one Spitalfields establishment which stands out from all the neighbouring competition, initially because of its large-scale, spectacular open grill, but then because of the personality of its tall, heavy-set American owner. 'Bubba' Hellberg wasn't actually known as Bubba until he came into the catering biz, but he really does come from Arkansas and, yes, he clearly remembers a time when he did once play Cowboys and Indians with a little boy named Billy Clinton, c.1951. ('Not Doctors and Nurses, thank God, or Kenneth Starr would have been on to me. I was jealous that Billy had a better cowboy suit than me.') Despite his slightly lugubrious, softly-spoken manner, Bubba soon proves to be a major raconteur, full of yarns about his years in the antique trade, his many travels around the States, a painful and expensive divorce ('When you get divorced in Baltimore, you open a bar so that you can pull') and his unexpected but gratifying sideways move from dealing antiques to broiling burgers and ribs. 'Fay Maschler says that these are the best burgers in London, God bless her, and so does Jonathan Meades, and who am I to contradict them?'

In addition to its thriving takeaway business — Richard is busy shooting pictures of the flames we had talked about earlier — Bubba's Arkansas Etc. has a back-room restaurant and bar, crammed to the gunwales with cheerfully corny Americana, including an Elvis-head trophy under a glass dome. Signs on the wall urge all visiting Americans to vote this crucial election year: Bubba may pose as a redneck, but he has nothing but contempt for the present incumbent of the White House, about whom he has an interesting medical theory that prudence forbids me to commit to print. Bubba's is, I suspect, one of the handful of joints I will be coming back to as a paying customer when our trip is done.

$\rightarrow$

The worst burger in town? See
Wimpy Bar, p.86

BEIGEL BAKE
BRICK LANE

This part of the East End has seen wave after wave of immigration in the last few centuries: refugee Huguenots — hence Fournier Street (home of Gilbert and George, the Morecambe and Wise of contemporary British art) — Eastern European and Russian Jewry, and peoples from the Indian subcontinent: first Bengalis (many initially employed in the then-Jewish-owned clothing industry) and then, after the end of the civil war in East Pakistan, 1971, Bangladeshis. Not so long ago, as recently as the 1960s, this area was still the main place for Londoners to come for the exotic treat of Jewish foods, both fast and slow. One guide book called it 'Saltbeefsville'. Its uncrowned king, or unchained lord mayor, was 'Tubby' Isaacs, shellfish-stall owner supreme. One of Tubby's most popular outlets was in Goulston Steet, Whitechapel, opposite the Hoop and Grapes pub.

In the same period, Wentworth Street, near the internationally famous Bloom's kosher restaurant — opened in 1952, closed in 1994 (another branch survived in Golders Green) — was identified by the *cognoscenti* as the place to go for London's best smoked salmon, with Old Montague Street a fierce competitor. The Jewish salt beef bars of this area were about last place you could hope to find that prole delicacy mentioned in an old Cockney anthem:

Boiled beef and carrots,
Boiled beef and carrots,
That's the stuff for your Derby Kell,
Makes you fit and keeps you well . . .

Derby Kell = Derby Kelly = Belly.
Today, the principal surviving trace of the Jewish residency is this bagel or beigel bar. In the early 1980s, I recall, it was a near-legendary purveyor of snacks to the hungry insomniac; nostalgists speak wistfully of how it felt to drive across miles of London for bleary-eyed ages so as finally to sink your teeth into a cream-cheese and smoked salmon bagel, or beigel, in the chill of the early hours. That experience seems so much a part of word-of-mouth London mythology

that you'd swear the shop had been here for centuries, and yet the staff seem proud enough to declare that it opened in 1976. Meanwhile, the sign on the competing bagel shop a couple of doors away brags of Victorian origins. Various locals deny this vehemently, and assure us that the 1976 place is the real deal, the kosher item.

Bagels aside, Brick Lane is now synonymous with one thing above all else: that mode of Asian nutrition which the British, riding roughshod over geopolitical and culinary exactitude alike, call either 'a curry' or 'an Indian'. (I have known visiting Americans look baffled or alarmed at the suggestion of 'going for an Indian', since it sounds to the unaccustomed ear far too much like an invitation to a lynch mob rather than a nice sit-down dinner.) Since 1998, Brick Lane has officially been designated as 'Banglatown'. London's Bangladeshi community, which accounts for fully half of the immigrants to the UK from that young country, is the largest outside Bangladesh itself. It's pretty much an open secret these days that a very large proportion of the so-called 'Indian' restaurants in Britain are actually Bangladeshi. The industry employs some 70,000 people, and has an annual turnover of £2 billion.

We are, in short, wandering through Curry Central.

→
More beigels already at **Bagel Factory**, *p.121*
Homage to curry at **Roxy**, *p.123*

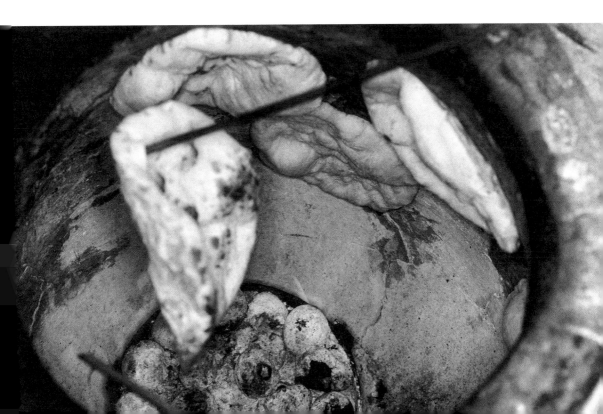

SALIQUE

BRICK LANE

'Under Strict Supervision of the Halal' says the sign on the window. Obviously, I know the adjectival use of 'halal' — opposite of 'haram', right? Means 'lawful' or 'permitted'? — but what exactly is THE Halal? Some kind of dietary council? When the Jewish restaurateurs and shopkeepers were here, the line between kosher and trifah was keenly policed by the Board for the Affairs of Shechta. Not everyone knows that.

CAFE BENGAL

BRICK LANE

Famous locally for its glowing oil portrait of Diana, Princess of Wales, by Kafait Hussain. The skin tone remains English Rose, but he has subtly and ingeniously modified her features — something around the nose, perhaps? — to give her a slightly more Asian appearance. She is the only English icon in the place — Hussain's other paintings are themes and variations from Indian mythology and its Bollywood restatements — so it feels as if some kind of syncretism is going on here, with Di taking her unexpected place in an expanded Indian pantheon. Everywhere we have gone, postcards of Princess Di have appeared above the counters and stoves: she has tacitly been elected the patron saint of British fast food outlets. A saint, evidently, for all faiths. It is strangely touching.

→

Follow the Diana memorial trail to **Wimpy**, *p.86*

BANOFUL MISHTI
BRICK LANE

A treasury of rich Indian sweetmeats, displayed in all their ravishing primary colours and in sparkling pastels of pink, yellow, green. Richard is enchanted.

More Indian sweetmeats at
***Raghuvanshi Sweets**, p.126*

YE FRYING PAN
BRICK LANE

A cultural palimpsest: spelled out in brick at the top of the building, the place's original name — presumably a late Victorian fish and chip shop? Jewish? — arranged around two brick frying pans, their handles crossed as in a heraldic achievement. Below, a sign declares the building's new identity: BALTI CUISINE.

KHUSHUBU TAKEAWAY
OSBORN STREET & WHITECHAPEL
HIGH STREET

In purely visual terms, this is perhaps the most remarkable fast food place we've found so far. For one thing, there's a large abstract painting on the wall: very New York loft. The walls are gleaming white, the tables are slate-grey, the chairs chrome and black, and the whole room is suffused by a blue light from overhead fluorescent strips. It is science-fiction clean, *Starship Enterprise* clean, so clean you could probably perform open-heart surgery here. And the mainly Asian clientele is all sharply dressed in suits and ties, ready for business, 21st-century style. Forget the three-hour, three-bottle business lunch: if your time really is money, then fast food is a shrewd investment of your lunch minutes. Gordon Gekko would have approved.

STARBUCKS
RUSSELL STREET, COVENT GARDEN

Do the owners know that this is the site of some of the earliest coffee houses in London: Button's, Will's and Tom's? Starbucks itself was founded in 1971, and grew only modestly for its first decade or so: by 1982 there was a total of just four branches, all in its home town, Seattle. Real growth only began in the later eighties, under the control of Howard Schultz, who bought the company out from his previous employers. By 1993 there were 275 branches, by 1996 a thousand. Schultz, quoted in the *Independent*, 24 May 2000:

'Our aim is to see more people drinking coffee than eating hamburgers. McDonald's has 25,000 outlets around the world . . . I don't like to draw comparisons with McDonald's, but we are going to get there too.'

The first London Starbucks was opened in the King's Road, Chelsea on 17 September 1998. A further 229 London outlets opened in the next four years, a small but significant fraction of the 5689 branches that had appeared across 28 countries by September 2002. Global sales in the previous year had reached $2.6 billion, profits $181.2 million.

$\rightarrow$

*For an alternative brew see **Lyons**, p.88*

A VERY BRIEF HISTORY OF LONDON'S COFFEE

The story of London's coffee consumption is so long, detailed and fascinating that it cries out for a study of its own. Fortunately, that cry has gone heeded by the freelance historian Antony Clayton, whose heavily illustrated and well-documented 2003 study, *London's Coffee Houses: A Stimulating Story*, performs the task admirably. I have freely plundered the following abbreviated chronology from his pages.

Sophisticated Londoners have known about coffee since the early seventeenth century, thanks to accounts by Francis Bacon (1627) and Robert Burton (in *The Anatomy of Melancholy*, 1621), but they only started to swill it — and its cousin, tea — after the Restoration. The coffee houses of the eighteenth century — the Bedford, Button's, Will's, the Spread Eagle and Tom King's in Covent Garden; The Chapter near St Paul's; Old Slaughter's in St Martin's Lane; White's in St James's; Garraway's, The Marine and Batson's in and near Cornhill; Don Saltero's in Chelsea — are probably too well known to need much more than a passing mention here, and their direct descendants, anyway, are not so much the Starbucksy high-street bars as the grander gentleman's clubs. Considered as a Fast Drink, coffee only comes into its own during the early nineteenth century, in response to two forms of socioeconomic pressure: the considerable reduction in import duty on coffee, and the growth of the Temperance movement, which was remarkably influential in weaning the British working man and his family away from beer and towards the cups that cheer but do not inebriate.

Some major stepping stones:

early to mid-1800s

Duty on British West Indian Coffee falls sharply from 1s 6d per pound in 1800 to 3d per pound in 1851. (Tea duty was relatively high until the 1840s, which was why coffee was the preferred national beverage of those decades. The cliché that the Englishman subsists on tea is of mid- to late-Victorian origin.)

c.1815 onwards

Origins of the 'coffee room', which provided the working classes with hot drinks, simple food, periodicals and warmth from about five in the morning to ten at night. After a slow start — it takes a while for workers to stop regarding coffee as a feeble, girlish, risible substitute for beer — they proliferate rapidly. By 1838 there are 332 registered coffee rooms; by 1843, nearly 2000. In 1853, the first of the Temperance Pubs is opened in Dundee; this innovative effort is taken up by the National Temperance League, which establishes a chain of 'British Workman Public Houses'.

1850s

Some 300 coffee stalls are by now plying their trade in

and around Hyde Park Corner, Charing Cross, the West India Docks and elsewhere. As pubs retreat before the Temperance attack, and opening times grow ever shorter, the coffee stand increasingly takes over as a reliable source of all-night drinks and snacks: cake, sandwiches, saveloys, hard-boiled eggs and the like.

1860s

The Aerated Bread Company — ABC — opens its first tea-shop in the Strand. Aimed more at the lower-middle-class white-collar worker and at 'respectable' women than at labourers, the ABC becomes a standard feature of British life. By 1893, London has 60 ABCs; by 1900, one hundred. In his poem *A Cooking Egg* (written 1917, published 1919), T.S. Eliot refers to souls weeping in a 'hundred' ABCs, to the frequent bafflement of later generations of readers. In his *Student's Guide to the Selected Poems* of T.S. Eliot, R.C. Southam devotes several scholarly paragraphs (pp.104-5) to elucidating the ABC reference: the shops were, it seems, great favourites with the Ezra Pound/Wyndham Lewis circle. Both Pound and Lewis made approving references to the chain in their own creative eruptions.

1920s/1930s

A fresh wave of Italian immigration gives birth to a British institution which thrives for decades, and even struggles into the 21st century: the cafe, otherwise known to locals as the Caff or Kayf. Standard fare at the caff: fry-ups, bangers and mash, fish and chips, gallons of tea.

1938

Swiss scientists at Nestlé devise the first adequately palatable instant coffee: Nescafé is born.

1953

Gina Lollobrigida, leading Italian sex symbol of her day, graces the opening of the Moka Bar at 29 Frith Street, Soho. The Moka boasts a Gaggia machine, the first ever seen in the UK; London discovers espresso and cappuccino. The Moka is also brightly decorated with a brand new material: Formica. Nothing will ever be the same.

1950s/1960s

The 'coffee bar' scene in Soho, a magnet for the young who have neither the money nor the legal right to drink in pubs, becomes the breeding ground for British pop and rock'n'roll.

1954

Arrival of the Wimpy Bar. See below.

1994

London's first internet cafe, Cyberia, at 39 Whitfield Street.

1998

Starbucks year. See above.

2001

Sixty per cent of the branded coffee market in the UK is controlled by just four chains: Starbucks, Costa Coffee, Coffee Republic, Caffe Nero.

2003

Five million espressos, cappuccinos, lattes and related beverages are sipped every week in the UK.

Clayton asserts that at the beginning of the 21st century, coffee was the second-fastest-growing UK market after that for mobile phones. But the chains started to lose profits badly during 2001 and 2002, partly as a result of job losses in the City of London. There are signs that the froth will continue to subside, especially as customers grow more aware of the huge mark-ups that many chains — especially Starbucks — are charging for a not particularly distinguished product. Popular American saying, used when trying to make someone aware of a potentially or actually disastrous state of affairs: 'Wake up, and smell the coffee.'

YASAR'S KEBABS
BLACKHORSE LANE, WALTHAMSTOW

Telling detail: the skewers here are not just the bog-standard knitting-needle lookalikes, but have highly ornate handles — Arabesques. Within a matter of minutes it is obvious that this is one of the best establishments of its kind we've seen, and exactly why: the whole family pitches in vigorously, from the monoglot grannies in their headscarves who sit hunched and chop salad stuff, to the slim, young men who run the grills and handle the customers; and though the work is hard and fairly relentless, they take pride in the quality of their food and the fact that almost all their business comes from regulars. 'I must know, what, 90 per cent of the people who come in here. I was at school with a lot of them,' says one of the young men ('I've got a Turkish name, but people call me Chris'). He has longish, unusually pale hair, which he keeps back not with the conventional chef's white cap but with a sort of metallic Alice band.

Chris tells us that the business was founded in 1976 by the late Mr Yasar, who had previously worked as a coach driver in his native country. 'When he came here from Trabazon, in the Black Sea area, he didn't speak a word of English. If he wanted a loaf of bread or something, he'd just have to point.' This chimes with something we've been meaning to investigate: the all but universal habit, in fast food joints, of displaying great big colour pictures of the fare on offer. I venture the assumption that these are designed to attract trade from people like the late Mr Yasar, who can't speak English, or from small children. Chris strongly doubts this: 'We put those up a few years ago and it really made a difference to sales. People like it. I mean, everyone knows what a burger is, right? But they'll still point to the picture of a burger and say, "I'll have one of them, please." You wanna see what you're eating . . .'

When Mr Yasar died, nine years ago, the family decided to carry on with the business he'd built up from next to nothing. 'It was tough in the first years, you'd sometimes get fights at night, but that's all changed for the better now. If we see trouble coming, we just lock the outer door, don't let the idiots in. No problem.'

The hours are long, but they're doing well enough to take holidays now and again, and Chris likes to go back to Turkey whenever he can. He's driven there and back a couple of times, and has tales of his impressions en route, sometimes fairly scathing: 'Romania — that's not a country, mate, that's a field. I'm telling you. All these old people, looking like they're straight out of Communism . . . Shocking!' His accent is such pure E17 that it almost comes as a shock when he breaks into Turkish to talk with a customer. Otherwise, he is your classic Cockney philosopher.

When we prompt him to muse a bit on his experiences of the fast food world, he makes a staunch defence of the kebab as the healthiest of all FF varieties, and explains the times needed for cooking. A lamb kebab takes about seven minutes to prepare. Chicken, because of the risk of salmonella poisoning, takes the longest — 'white meat, that'll slaughter you'. But loyalty to the kebab trade doesn't keep him out of McDonald's. He gives us a couple of *gratis* mineral waters, leans over the counter and stares out onto the street.

'I dunno,' he says. 'Life, eh?'

→

*Kebabs Southall style at **Asian Kebab**, p.128*

DIGRESSION: ON THE MEDIEVAL KEBAB

A few years ago, the freelance historian Robert Chenciner purported to have found a scene in the Bayeux Tapestry of knights frying up Gazza's favourite. This prompted a cartoon in the *Evening Standard* of one armoured medieval warrior saying to another, 'Fancy a kebab?'

NIN COM SOUP

ST ANNE'S WELL, OLD STREET UNDERGROUND PRECINCT

We blunder across this remarkable place entirely by accident, en route to check out the plethora of kebab joints on the road towards Hoxton. The interior is as large as a warehouse, with spare, bare walls partially but eccentrically decorated — another rare breath of Manhattan. On the far wall is a large yellow painting based on a Victorian exercise book for gentlemen; to the right, a wall that appears to be covered with the kind of flock wallpaper standard in tandoori restaurants in the 1970s. Furniture includes a long church pew and an antique leather couch, while . . .

Oh yes, the food. Nin Com Soup specializes in thick, edible liquids, both hot and cold — soups and broths, as the whimsical name implies, but also a range of juices. The particular gimmick here is that you can choose the raw materials of your beverage, neatly prepacked in a plastic bag; you take your selection to the counter, and the server mixes it with a little crushed ice and puts it through a sort of mini-cyclotron doohickey. I opt for a combo of apples, lemon and fresh ginger. The resulting slush is a little too intensely flavoured, what with the heat of the ginger and the tartness of the citrus, but it leaves you feeling both refreshed and smug, an unbeatable sensation.

This place needs further investigation, so we decide to hang around for a while until the manager returns. His name, it emerges, is Ben Page-Philips; he's 35, used to work in the wine trade for Corney & Barrow, and set this place up with his brother Tom, selling off their shared house to raise the venture capital. It was a slow process, with heavy outlays on equipment and minimal returns, and for a while Ben and Tom had to live on the premises: 'Not many people live in the middle of a roundabout.' They opened in 2001, and the business is now doing well enough for them to start thinking of modest expansion. 'You know that Soup Opera has gone into receivership? We've been looking at one or two of their places, to see if we might be able to adapt them.'

The New York-ish look of the place isn't a fluke: Ben has worked as a chef in various parts of the US, including a posh eatery in Santa Fe, and he checked out the juice bar business both there and in Australia. Nin Com Soup isn't exactly the first of its kind in the UK, but as far as Ben knows it's the first to use the expensive high-tech machinery he's bought in from overseas, and the first to use the buy-in-the-bag fruit and veg procedure.

We wish him well as we leave, and mean it.

Pulp Facts in **Crussh***, p.115 and p.117*

WIMPY BAR
LONDON ROAD, MORDEN

'A CORNERSTONE of the British way of life' — definition of the Wimpy Burger from the company's website, www.wimpyburgers.co.uk

We have come to Morden, the most southerly outpost of the Northern Line, in hope of finding almost extinct species of fast food joint, and within seconds of leaving the station our hopes are gratified. A Wimpy Bar!

(This snotty response, this smug and nasty assumption that the Wimpy chain must be in a state of near-extinction, is self-evidently nothing more than effete middle-class Southern prejudice. There are, it seems on further investigation, some 300 Wimpy outlets currently operating throughout the UK — a healthy figure which, the company website boasts, makes Wimpy the country's largest single operator of franchise restaurants.

But, let's be honest: when did you last notice one?)

For a generation of Britons, the baby-boom generation now entering the nursery slopes of old age or middle-middle age, a Wimpy Burger is the high-fat, low-fibre counterpart of Proust's madeleine, the greasy taste of a lost childhood world. Actually, it's a lot more than that: it's a memory of how an impoverished, enforcedly austere Britain tried to respond to the rumours of popular affluence, youthfulness and FUN!!! that were filtering back from over the Atlantic, and did so in a half-arsed, miserably, wretchedly, embarrassingly wrong way. America had Elvis, Jerry Lee Lewis and Burger King; we had Cliff Richard, Tommy Steele and the Wimpy.

Oh, the shame — largely retrospective shame, mind, since at the time the Wimpy Bars, launched in 1954 (after a trial run at the Ideal Home Exhibition in 1953), were a roaring success among the new species known as 'teenagers'.

Richard and I are joined today by a bona fide American, Professor Martin Wallen, author of *City of Health, Fields of Disease* (Ashgate, 2004) and keen amateur student of English folkways. It doesn't take him, or us, long to note how enthusiastically Wimpy ('Celebrating 50 Years, 1954-2004') is selling itself as above all a purveyor of staunchly patriotic fare. Their counterpart to the Big Mac is 'The Best of British — Double Decker', advertised on posters which juxtapose their two-tier burger with an old-style two-tier London bus. The plastic menu cards are festooned with regulation British signifiers, from cricketers on the village green to Stonehenge, the Houses of Parliament, a red post box . . . and, incongruously modernistic element, Antony Gormley's (in my view, rather fine) *Angel of the North* statue. Remarkable, this inclusion, when you recall how much spleen and derision attended its earliest days from the usual reactionary quarters. Incidentally, the Wimpy counterpart to Ronald McDonald is a cute little cartoon Beefeater with a big nose.

Wimpy was founded by the giant catering business J. Lyons and Co. A little background is in order.

THE RISE AND FALL OF THE HOUSE OF LYONS: A LIGHTNING HISTORY

For almost a century, J. [for Joe or Joseph] Lyons and Co. was the most prominent catering business in the UK; unlike the Wimpyburger, it genuinely did have some claim to being a CORNERSTONE of the British Way of Life. It began in Newcastle in 1887, when Joseph Lyons (1847-1917) joined forces with three colleagues to provide catering for that city's Royal Jubilee Exhibition. This proved so successful that they went on to cater for similar exhibitions in Glasgow and Paris. In 1894, J. Lyons was set up as a public company, moved into grand premises at Cadby Hall, and opened the first of more than 200 Lyons teashops at 214 Piccadilly. By 1895, the company was already prominent enough to win a contract to cater for manoeuvres by the Brigade of Guards.

It is hard to exaggerate the scale and influence of the Lyons operation in the first half of the twentieth century.

They introduced the British public to frozen foods; they built the world's first business computer, LEO (Lyons Electronic Office) and went on to supply computers for others; they bought out existing brands from Findus and Baskin-Robbins to Tetley's tea and Dunkin' Donuts. They owned tea estates in the Far East and factories at home, ran laundries and printing works, established grand restaurants including the Trocadero in Shaftesbury Avenue, employed so many musicians that they set up their own Orchestral Department. The uniformed tea-shop waitresses, known as Nippies, became a British stereotype recognized almost everywhere. The Lyons chain of hotels included the Regent Palace, in its day the largest in Europe. Another of their hotels, the Cumberland at Marble Arch, was — astonishing fact — built by the company's own works department. In the Second World War they made bombs and DIY military bridges, as well as supplying rations for troops and the Red Cross.

Like other empires, Lyons once seemed immortal. Like other empires, it perished mainly from overweening ambition. In the early 1970s, the company borrowed some $100,000,000 — mainly from US sources — and rapidly bought out nine other food companies around the world. The global oil crisis of 1973 put paid to all that, and one by one their assets were sold off to meet rapidly accelerating, and ultimately crushing debts — Wimpy went to United Biscuits in 1976. In 1978, the 91-year-old company was taken over by Allied Breweries. By 1998, nothing of the old Lyons remained. *Sic transit gloria mundi.*

The first Wimpy bar was opened in the basement of a Lyons tea shop at 277 Oxford Street in May 1954. (By 1969 there were no fewer than 461 Wimpy franchises across the nation.) Lyons also targeted the lucrative new youth market with other chains, notably the Golden Egg, and the occasional one-off, such as Chips With Everything at 88 Chancery Lane. An article on 'Teenagers' by Jane Wilson (b. 1939) in Len Deighton's *London Dossier* (1967) explained that it

'. . . serves automated permutations of eggs, beans, sausages, bacon and chips. The decor was conceived, according to the designer [Michael Wollf, of Main Wolff and Partners] in terms of a "pin-table aesthetic" — so everything is neon-lit in combinations of egg yellow, ketchup red and electric blue, and deafening music is provided by a giant jukebox. This is where the working City mod goes for his mid-day transfusion of R'n B.' (Len Deighton added a downbeat PS: 'The restaurant is closing as we go to press.' L.D.)

Richard orders a pint (!) of Coke and a Burger meal. I order a coffee (which turns out to be UK default standard: frothy hot water adulterated with something vaguely milky and something faintly bitter — not nice). Professor Wallen, sensibly, orders nothing, simply looks bemused. We all note the inevitable postcard of Princess Diana above the counter. The Burger meal arrives. The Wimpy itself is a small, flat, greyish-brown disc topped with a thin paste of finely chopped off-white onion. Wallen, used to ample American portions, is aghast:
    'Christ! That's smaller than my penis!'
    How is it? we ask, as Richard eats.
    'Horrible.'

→

Follow the Diana memorial trail to
***Cafe Diana**, p.96*

MORDEN CAFE RESTAURANT
LONDON ROAD, MORDEN

The proprietor, who says that we should call him 'Key' ('It's my nickname'), is initially so keen for publicity that he starts to art-direct Richard's shoot, and bamboozles a couple of middle-aged women customers to pose grinning through the window. But when Richard asks if he can photograph inside, it's clear that our welcome is at an end. For the nth time, we wonder: why the change of attitude? What's the anxiety?

TOOTING BROADWAY
VARIOUS OUTLETS AND A PUB

Thrown into reminiscent mode by the chance encounter with Wimpy, I propose that we check out developments in Tooting, my home district when I was between the ages of three and eleven. Well, that American guy (Thomas Wolfe, not Martin Wallen) was right: You Can't Go Home Again. I am quite literally incapable of recognizing anything here, except maybe the public library and what appear to be the remains of the old ABC cinema. Gone, certainly, is the covered market, where the sight of eels threshing around while the fishmonger hacked them into bloody chunks (some eerie neurological freak kept the chunks twisting for what seemed ages) was a weekly source of horror.

We could be anywhere in unfashionable London. Apart from the many curry houses — not our brief, though rumour has it that the quality is high in Tooting — it's the usual McD, Pizza H, BK, KFC, and a slew of independents so nondescript and unappealing that, come lunchtime and the need to eat for sustenance rather than research, we end up ordering BLTs in a pub. Served by a burly man in camouflage trousers and combat boots, festooned with tattoos and body piercings, but possessed of a surprisingly delicate manner and light voice. And they're really quite good, these baguette sandwiches, made with juicy slices of back bacon instead of the usual near-desiccated shards of streaky. I have nothing much to observe about this, save for wishing to record the greatly improved standards of pub grub in my lifetime, and the rareness, nowadays, of finding a pub in which the food is anything like as crummy as it is in the worst fast food joints.

THE FISHCOTHEQUE
NEAR WATERLOO STATION

One of London's most famous fish bars, strongly
recommended to me by Dr Harry Rutter of
Oxford University. An outré rock combo, The Jazz
Butcher, once wrote a song about it. There's a
slightly retro feel about the decor, a fifties look,
of which the capstone is a small aquarium of
bright tropical fish in the far left-hand corner.
A smartly dressed man in his late sixties or
thereabouts — cufflinks, tie and breast pocket
handkerchief — comes in for a late lunch of his
favourite dish here, a couple of deep-fried
saveloys and chips. 'It's all kebabs and rubbish
like that nowadays,' he grumbles, though he
proves to be much less of a curmudgeon than
his growl and scowl suggest.

*Posh fish and chips at **Geale's**, p.97*

ON THE SAVELOY

The name is said to come from the Spanish *cervelas*, itself from the French *cervelles*, 'brains', since brains were originally a major component of this long sausage, in combination with pork meat, pork fat, garlic and pepper. It could be eaten either smoked or unsmoked: cooked in hot water and served with vegetables, or fried, or eaten cold as part of a salad. Catholic countries experimented for a while with a meat-free version using pike, eggs and potatoes, suitable for consumption by the pious in Lent. By Dickens's time, the saveloy was a well-established favourite of the urban proletariat, 'a standard item of street-side fast-food' (Tames, 2003). Saltpetre was added to its meaty contents to stop them from rotting, and turned the saveloy a familiar bright red colour. Its phallic appearance launched a thousand bawdy jokes in the music halls.

Our saveloy connoisseur's name is Dennis, 'two ns', and he tells us that he served for 25 years in the Metropolitan Police, based mainly around here in Waterloo and other parts of South London. He took a fair bit of violence in the course of his career — ribs broken, teeth kicked out. 'If you get through your service without that, you're either very lucky or you're the type who stands back.' He did his National Service in the Royal Artillery, was lucky enough never to see battle, and on leaving the Army trained as an engineer, 'but I could see the way the British economy was going' — the collapse of traditional heavy industries — 'and joined the police instead'.

You'd probably guess that Dennis is the sort of chap who'd have pretty tough views on most law and order issues, and you'd probably not be far wrong, but on one point at least he's right there with mainstream liberal opinion. As a member of the IPA, the International Police Association, he managed to see a lot of what has been happening in continental Europe, and he considers that the arming of Italian policeman on the beat has been 'a disaster — first step on a slippery slope'.

The restaurant is otherwise empty, so I leave Dennis to enjoy his meal in peace and fall into conversation with the men behind the counter. Up on the wall, next to the Pukka pie signs, are some rather handsome Islamic icons, 'from Istanbul'. Very beautiful, I say. 'This one is the 99 names of God,' the head cook explains to me, a little shyly, 'and this one is the beginning of the Koran.' I find it quite charming to think of how much fried food is being served to Londoners under the Holy name of Allah, the Compassionate, the Merciful.

A fashionably dressed young girl comes in — Alicia, from Spain. Alicia is ready enough to pose for Richard's camera, but wants to know what our project is all about. Fast food in London, Richard says. She ponders.

'You mean bad food?'

CAFE DIANA
NOTTING HILL GATE

Since the death of the Princess in 1997, this modest supplier of coffees, fizzy drinks and (mainly) Arabian-style snacks has become something of an unofficial shrine. Diana really did drop in here from time to time, it seems, and there is at least one framed, signed letter to 'Dear Abdul', thanking him for the 'lovely flowers' he sent her as a birthday present. The walls are packed with photographs and press cuttings; there must be easily a hundred images of her. Today, it seems more than a tad depressing to see so many smiling representations of this sad young woman, unaware of the Reaper waiting just a couple of feet offstage.

CHOPSTIX
QUEENSWAY

A sudden hunger attack, late in the afternoon, and only £5.50 in loose change between us. It stretches to a couple of vegetable spring rolls and a nondescript curry-ish sludge which might once have been based on chicken. Our joint blood sugar is so low that we slurp it all down greedily and want more.

The murals in this place are large and lurid and just a shade cryptic — in the Manga style, to my inexpert eye. Quite striking, but the staff won't let us take photographs. The hell with them. We're not coming here again.

GEALES
NOTTING HILL GATE

Geales is surely the classic London instance of a restaurant taking up a tasty proletarian staple — viz. fish and chips — and representing it, suitably modified, to the bourgeoisie. Countless Italian restaurants have performed a roughly similar trick, persuading affluent Britons to pay top whack for food that a Tuscan auto mechanic might consider a trifle elementary, but remarkably few have successfully applied it to our humblest native cuisines. Anyone for designer Yorkshire Pud? Spotted Dick? Prunes and Custard?

The historico-social quirks of this admittedly excellent eatery are magnified tonight by the fact that one of our party, in exuberant damn-the-expense mood, calls for a dozen oysters as a starter. Oysters: surely the most extreme case in all culinary history of a once-despised foodstuff miraculously transformed into a treat for the rich and snobbish?

In 1701, you could buy 200 oysters for 4 shillings — that is, for 20p, or 10 for 1p. (Source: *A Collection of Bills, Accounts, and Inventories*, 1650-1750, ed. J.O. Halliwell, 1852.) Hucksters sold them from street barrows, with gilt gingerbread. Workers used to have it written into their conditions of employment that they would not be fed on oysters, because oysters were too cheap. Tobias Smollett (*The Expedition of Humphrey Clinker*, 1771) refers to the practice of keeping oysters for days in 'slime pits' covered with 'vitriolic scum', to give them the green colour which punters found particularly appealing.

Then there is the famous digression by Dickens's Sam Weller:

'. . . poverty and oysters always seem to go together . . . the poorer a place is the greater call there seems for oysters . . . Look here, sir, here's a oyster-stall to every half-dozen houses [in Whitechapel]. The street's lined vith 'em. Blessed if I don't think that ven a man's wery poor, he rushes out of his lodgings, and eats oysters in reg'lar desperation.'

As late as 1840, oysters still cost only 4d a dozen, but:

'. . . within a very few years they were so dear as to be a luxury only the wealthy could afford. There is little doubt that the cause of this rise in price was reckless dredging of the natural beds as a result of increasing demand from the rapidly expanding towns. Had it not been that something was known by this time of the breeding habits of oysters, and of methods of cultivating them artificially, the mollusc might have become almost extinct in English waters.' (Drummond & Wilbraham, p.309)

After the dozen Geales oysters, most of us order cod, chips and — of course — mushy peas, washed down with red wine (no James Bond nonsense about only white with fish tonight). Somebody reminds us of the amusing occasion when Peter Mandelson dropped in at a fish'n'chip shop for a quick photo-opportunity, and, seeing a tray of mushy peas, asked for 'some of that guacamole'. Laughs all round. A couple of the more robust diners indulge in puddings.

The bill for six, including service, comes to £253.

$\rightarrow$

An urban fish and chip legend at
Micky's, p.135

THE SCOTTISH RESTAURANT (1): GIVING THE DEVIL HIS DUE

Warning to readers:
This section has temperate and even approving things to say about the McDonald's Corp.

McDONALD'S
NOTTING HILL GATE

'And the merry clowns, the Big Mac signs, the colourful, unique decorations and ideal cleanliness — all of this complements the hamburgers whose great popularity is well deserved.'
Mikhail Gorbachev, 1999

A potentially traumatic moment. My first time inside a McDonald's since 23 December 1986. I was working late at the old BBC offices in Kensington House, near Shepherd's Bush Green. Everywhere else was closed. I seem to recall that I ordered a Big Mac. Whatever it was, it tore through my innards and exited within less than two hours, though that was not the fault of the global chain, but of a tuna salad I'd eaten in Morocco several days earlier, which gave me the worst food poisoning I have ever experienced. The Big Mac itself I recall as excessively sweet and a bit slimy, served in a pappy, sugary white roll which offered no resistance to the teeth. Not exactly disgusting, but not something you'd want to eat regularly.

As you already know, sagacious Reader, there are all sorts of reasons for persons of goodwill to despise McDonalds, and wish its outlets consigned to bottomless perdition. I will be rehearsing them with (sugar-free) relish in just a while. First, though, some unaccustomed cheerfulness and light: one or two favourable things you can say about McDonald's.

Above all: about the toilets. Some people have told me that there are McDonald's toilets which are fiercely policed — admission by key or code, strictly for the paying customer — but at least one (former) young mother insisted that I serve the cause of truth by pointing out how invaluable McDonald's had been as a pee- or pooh-station when her (now adult) daughter was under five. Clean and reliable lavatories and baby-changing stations are, she continued, notoriously hard to find in London, and the sheer ubiquity of McDonald's added greatly to the quality of life in our capital.

Other good things that people have said about McDonald's:

- Job creation (crew level).
- Introduces teenagers to work disciplines; gives them a measure of financial independence.
- Wealth creation (franchisee level).
- Cleanliness, especially of lavatories, has knock-on effect: introduction of higher standards of general lavatory cleanliness in, for example, Hong Kong.
- Safety for customers, especially women customers, who often appreciate the fact that their local McDonald's does not serve alcohol and thus attract boozy, nasty men.
- Genuine boon to local economies, not only via employment but by sensitively sourcing many products from local slaughterhouses, wheat farms, dairies etc.
- Quiet, air-conditioned and thus conducive to serious study (parts of Asia only).
- Daytime refuge for the homeless (depending on management policy).
- Cheap (in some markets).
- Extremely cheap. (Ditto.)
- Highly effective for pacifying otherwise unruly children. Absolute familiarity, profoundly soothing for the homesick traveller and reassuring for the timid ones.
- Swift, thorough and conscientious reaction to single-issue protests, e.g. African-American complaints about discriminatory franchising policies in the late 1960s; abandonment of polystyrene boxes in the United States (1990) in response to Green activists.
- Fun!
- Cool!

An interesting omission from this list of ticks: it is not very often said that the food is delicious, or good, or even acceptably palatable for adults. (Though honesty compels me to report that Jeffery Steingarten, no less an authority, seems very fond of McDonald's fare, particularly the French fries — 'excellent' — and writes quite lyrically of his visit to the Wall Street branch at 160 Broadway: see 'Staying Alive' in *The Man Who Ate Everything*.) In parts of Asia, many customers have had to learn to suppress a reaction of disgust to the presence of cheese in some products; and many regular customers of McDonald's in Beijing admitted to interviewers that they did not like the unfamiliar Western tastes at all. What they were buying was an experience, an instant fantasy of Western life, modernity, cosmopolitanism, and glamour (!), not a meal.

It is certainly hard to feel that this branch in Notting Hill represents anything very sinister — any of the horrors so frequently cited in the anti-McD propaganda, from the promotion of gross obesity to vile labour practices. The clientele is youngish, no more than commonly plump, and fairly quiet. It is a clean, well-lit place, decorated in pastel tones of blue, grey and pinky-brown, with inoffensive if immediately forgettable pastel paintings scattered among the more garish posters, and — ah, yes; inescapable — the revolting leer of Ronald McDonald.

RONALDIANA

In *Fast Food Nation*, Eric Schlosser offers an abbreviated history of how this red-mouthed fiend was conjured from the deepest pits of Hell. The company's initial mascot was Speedee, a miniature cartoon chef with a hamburger where his head should be; but since Alka-Seltzer already had a mascot called Speedy, and especially since it was deemed wise to avoid any hint that consumption of the one product called for consumption of the other, Speedee was re-Christened Archie McDonald — presumably because 'Archie' alludes to the Golden Arches.

Came the fateful year of 1960. Oscar Goldstein, a McDonald's franchisee in the nation's capital, decided to sponsor a local children's television show, *Bozo's Circus*. When the actor who played Bozo (Willard Scott, later quite well known as an NBC weatherman) made personal appearances at the franchise, children and their parents turned up by the regiment. Three years later, when NBC cancelled the programme, Goldstein asked Scott to collaborate with an advertising agency and come up with a new clown to make further personal appearances. It was Scott who coined the name Ronald McDonald. In 1965, the Corporation made Ronald nationally famous through a major ad campaign, but Scott was no longer allowed to play the role: he was considered overweight. To this day, R McD is slim and *sportif*, and the McDonald's sponsorship ads for NBC's Olympic broadcasting in the summer of 2004 showed Ronald throwing weights, and executing a dazzling jump into a pool from the high board. Hah!

Perhaps in response to the McDonald's-bashing documentary *Supersize Me*, the Notting Hill Gate branch is pushing the 'healthy' salad option very strongly this week. (Spoilsport journalists in the broadsheets have been pointing out that if you glop all the McDressing that is offered into your green leaves, you're going to be absorbing truly silly amounts of sugar and fat — as much, they say, as lurks in a Big Mac Meal.) In the window, other posters announce a charitable tie-in with the Football Association ('F.A. Community Shield') and thus send the message that the corporation heartily endorses healthy levels of sporting activity in the young. You have to concede the shrewdness, even while you cringe at the hypocrisy.

Richard, who has just arrived from photographing some local flower ladies tucking into their Burger King purchases, notes how brilliantly lit the backstage area of the kitchen is: 'They're saying, "We've got nothing to hide",' and analyzes the visual design of the place in terms of a universal principle which is taught to photographic beginners: that an intense light set to the rear of the image's planes will, so to speak, draw the viewer right in through the frame. As in those visions of the afterlife reported by survivors of near-death experiences, a McDonald's customer is being silently paged to 'come into the light'.

I find myself feeling rather nervous while queuing up to be served at the counter, like the only member of a stage company who has not learned his lines properly, and feel that there is something less than composed and businesslike about the way I place my order. It has often been noted that when a McDonald's opens in virgin territory, the company has to 'train' its new customers as well as its new workforce. Most importantly, the customer has to learn the implicit contract that fast food means fast consumption as well as fast production: it is your duty to eat efficiently, clear your tray and leave promptly, rather than linger for hours and block the tables that others wish to use. (But, as we have seen, the US 11-minute average mealtime is seldom attained in most overseas markets.) The training of customers extends to other areas, too.

When the Moscow branch opened, a woman with a bullhorn stood outside and bellowed, 'The employees inside will smile at you. This does not mean that they are laughing at you. We smile because we are happy to serve you.' Pictorial handouts explained the nature of every meal, with its assorted raw materials in the background, and told newcomers how to order, how to pay, and what to do when you were handed your tray of food. (On this business of smiling: McDonald's had to give way on the otherwise compulsory smile policy in certain parts of Asia. In China, a merchant who smiles at you as he takes your money is widely held to be swindling you. Elsewhere, the sight of employees smiling sends the message that they are mucking around and not taking their jobs seriously. Earnestness is now permitted as a legitimate local substitute.)

There is also a widespread belief in Hong Kong that it was McDonald's which taught people how to queue (though other accounts say that the practice was already creeping into standard HK behaviour in the years before McDonald's came), instead of pushing and shoving like members of a rugby scrum, as they certainly did when the first branch opened in 1975. In Beijing, Taiwan and other markets, customers initially refused to bus their own tables, since they regarded McDonald's as being like a formal restaurant, and only picked up the practice by imitating foreigners. Fashionable young Chinese people today say that they feel they are being more 'civilized', *wenming*, when they clear their own rubbish, because they understand that this is the appropriate etiquette. It's also been noticed that the Chinese speak more quietly than usual when inside McDonald's, litter much less outside, spit less and generally behave in a more polite manner. To those used to watching English oiks spitting and littering, this seems, let us say, counter-intuitive.

The teenage-ish girl behind the counter who serves me is efficient enough, but has only an imperfect command of English, so that we have to double-check each other's meanings. The food arrives from backstage in slightly less than a minute, and she urges me to 'enjoy', but says nothing about what she hopes for the rest of my day.

After almost two decades of abstinence (and I'd not exactly been a regular McDonald's punter before then, either) the prospect of eating the classic product seems too much like a jump in from the deep end, so while Richard has a medium burger, medium fries and a medium chocolate milkshake, I opt for a Crispy Chicken Ranch Salad (pushed as the very lowest of the low-cal option) and a small Minute Maid orange juice (Minute Maid is owned by the Coca-Cola Corporation). Total for the two of us: £7.45. My order accounts for about two-thirds of the cost.

How does it stack up? On the palatability front, moderately well: the lettuce is crisp, fresh and plentiful, if a little flavourless, the tomatoes ditto. There appears to be a minimal presence of cheese (taste: almost imperceptible), and possibly some tiny shards of ham. The creamy dressing is actually quite pleasant, but, mindful of the calorie warnings, I use only about a third of my sachet. The strips of chicken themselves are fine for what they are — about the size of plump match-sticks, and cooked in a tasty enough spicy crust. But there are very few of them, and the meal leaves me still feeling hungry. Richard is happier with his choice, voting his burger 'miles better than Wimpy's' and his milkshake 'great'. Unlike me, he's also happy with the value for money: 'When I leave a McDonald's, I always feel that I've come out with a quid more in my pocket.'

We are being joined for the next few hours by the poet, publisher and teacher Peter Carpenter. Among his many other accomplishments, Pete is the author of *The League Goals of Alan J. Pinkney*, a hilarious mock-epic about the fortunes of Crystal Palace F.C. rendered in the style of assorted lugubrious poems by T.S. Eliot, from *The Waste Land* to *Four Quartets*.

The dripping Bovril our only drink
The bloody hotdog our only food.

Pete and his wife have two young daughters, who have never, ever eaten in McDonald's. 'We call it "the Scottish restaurant", and make fun of it whenever possible. We've trained them to like Pizza Express.'

(Pedantic point: the McDonald brothers — Richard and Maurice, or Dick and Mac — actually traced their ancestry back to Ireland, not Scotland. Ray A. Kroc, the man who built the Empire — its true founder, on 2 March 1955 — was from Oak Park, Illinois by birth and doesn't seem to have talked much about his deep family background. Their story has been told many times — for a readable example, see *McDonald's Behind The Arches* by John F. Love.) Peter looks up at the figure of Ronald McDonald.

'So despicable,' he mutters.

THE SCOTTISH RESTAURANT (2):
THE DEVIL AND ALL HIS WORKS

Warning to readers:
There is little information in this section which
cannot be found in Eric Schlosser's Fast Food
Nation *and other polemics. If you haven't read*
Schlosser, please do so. But I will try to con-
dense some key points from his book-length
arguments into a handy, bite-size pasquinade,
hold the mayo, and throw in some extra sneers
of my own for the heck of it.

The McDonald's corporation is grotesquely litigious, so much so that they'll probably try to sue you if you say as much, and one must therefore tread carefully here, especially in the wake of the McLibel case, in which — remember? — two impoverished British Greenpeace activists were sued for distributing a pamphlet alleging that the company was guilty, *inter alia*, of destroying the Amazon rain forests, exploiting and creating poverty in the Third World, torturing animals and maltreating workers. Justice Roger Bell, who presided over the McLibel trial, found that the accused had failed to substantiate many of these charges, and thus, by the harsh rules of British libel law, were guilty as charged.

However: Justice Bell also found that the Greenpeace Two had satisfactorily documented their contention that the company endangered the health of customers who ate their products too frequently (i.e., several times a week), paid unreasonably low wages, and bore responsibility for cruelty to animals by some of its meat suppliers. The trial also turned up some facts unknown to the two, including acts of espionage by McDonald's hirelings and the active — and scandalous — participation of Special Branch in monitoring these 'subversives'. The case went to appeal, and on 31 March 1999, a group of three justices overruled parts of the earlier judgement, ruling that it was indeed accurate to claim that an excess of McDonald's in the diet causes heart disease, and that allegations of workers being treated badly amounted to 'fair comment'. (For further details, see John Vidal, *McLibel: Burger Culture on Trial*.) In February 2005, the European Court of Human Rights upheld a secondary appeal on the issue of legal aid.

There are many, many other objections that can and have been made against McDonald's. One of my favourites (because, though I am sure others have said it endlessly, I made it up for myself) is that it demonstrates how the old economic principle of Gresham's law applies to burgers as well as to currency — bad money drives out good. One can easily understand why McDonald's might have come as a force of culinary liberation in the land of the old British Rail Sandwich, but in Italy? in

China? in Japan? (to mention just three cultures where the peasant cuisine is famously healthy and the high cuisine generally exquisite). Cringe before the power of advertising, ye wretched of all nations!

Of all the charges that can be laid against the corporation, surely the least disputable is that it has, with undeniable efficiency and even brilliance, seduced the very young into craving its plainly unwholesome offerings. A study carried out by the McDonald's Corp in 1996 established that 96 per cent of American children could identify their Prince of Darkness, Ronald McDonald. (Chinese children appear to be catching up apace: 'All the children said they liked Ronald because he was funny, gentle, kind, and — several added — he understood children's hearts.' — Yunxiang Yan, *McDonald's in Beijing*.)

In a morbidly funny sequence of *Supersize Me*, a cross-section of American moppets all fail to identify an image of Jesus Christ (one tot, maybe a satirist in the making, hilariously haz-ards that it might be George W. Bush), and George Washington also draws several blanks, but they all know Ronald, and just what Ronald does.

That same 1996 study determined that exactly the same percentage of the total US popu-lation, 96 per cent, had eaten at a McDonald's at least once; on the average day, 8 per cent of the population will buy a McDonald's product. Now, apologists for the McEmpire are obviously quite right to say that the obesity epidemic which started to take off in the 1970s cannot be wholly blamed on the fast food chains.

Americans, and the rest of the affluent world, are simply becoming more and more sedentary, under-exercised and just plain bone idle. Fault: ours. However, it is equally undeni-able that a diet of fast food will pump you full of sugars and fats, starve you of fibres, and generally make you not merely gross but, unless you have a freakish metabolism, very unhealthy. Schlosser:

'. . . the major chains have apparently decided that it's much easier and much more profitable to increase the size and fat content of their portions than to battle eating habits largely

KILLER FAT: SOME QUICK REMINDERS

USA

- The USA now has the worst obesity rates in the world.
- More than half of American adults, and a quarter of American children, are medically classified as either (i) overweight, (ii) obese (about 44 million slobs), or (iii) super-obese (which means that six million Americans, the mega-slobs, each weigh some 100 pounds or more in excess of a normal, reasonable body mass).
- About 280,000 Americans die prematurely each year from obesity and directly related conditions: heart disease, cancers of the colon and stomach, diabetes, strokes and so on. Health care costs for obesity-related illness currently run at about $240 billion. This is not a good thing.

UK

- The UK now has the worst obesity rates in Western Europe.
- We also (surprise, eh?) eat more fast food than the rest of Western Europe.
- Between 1984 and 1993, the number of fast food outlets in the UK approximately doubled.
- So did obesity rates. (Coincidence?) This, too, is not a good thing. To be sure, it is not only — perhaps not even mainly — the burgers, fries and pizzas at the fast food joints that are turning us into a generation of lard-arses.

KILLER SUGARS: LIQUID SWEETIES

(I have Anglicized this sub-heading from a 1999 study by the American Center for Science in the Public Interest, entitled 'Liquid Candy'. And I prefer the antiquated English term 'fizzy drink' or 'fizz' to the American 'soda'.)
A few more scare stats:

- The average can of sweet fizzy drink contains the equivalent of ten teaspoons of sugar.
- Americans drink about 56 gallons of fizz per capita per annum; that is, roughly 600 twelve-ounce cans.
- Coca-Cola wishes to hike its sales by at least 25 per cent each year. Since the adult market is pretty much saturated, this means more aggressive targeting of adolescents and children, not only via the box and so on but in schools. (About 30 per cent of public high schools in the USA offer branded fast food; so do some elementary schools.) The ideal trainee consumer will be 8 years old.

- In 1978, the average American teenage boy drank about 7 ounces of fizzy drinks every day; by 1999, that intake had risen to about 20 ounces. This accounts for some 9 per cent of his daily calorific intake. Girls, who used to drink about 6 ounces, now consume about 12.

- Approximately 20 per cent of American toddlers are regularly given fizz by (presumably) well-intentioned but (shockingly) ignorant parents. (Don't feel smug about this, British reader; there have been reliable reports of Scottish mums giving their bairns Irn-Bru in the confident belief that it is a health drink.) Some of this is guzzled from baby bottles marked with the logos of Pepsi, Dr Pepper and Seven-Up.

- All fast food joints benefit handsomely from the sale of fizz, which has far and away the highest profit margin of any fast food product. Coke sells its syrup to the chains at roughly $4.25 a gallon. A medium Coke, retailing at $1.29, contains about 9 cents' worth of the sweet sludge. A large Coke, at $1.49, contains another 3 cents' worth. *Comme on dit* in America: you do the math.

- McDonald's sells more Coca-Cola than any other outlet. In the 1950s, an average fizz was about 8 ounces; today, a 'Child' Coke is 12 ounces, and a 'Large' 32 ounces — about 310 calories.

The horror! The horror!

SUSHI NOTO
AT CHAMBERLAIN'S, LEADENHALL MARKET

Pete Carpenter used to work as a City messenger many years ago, and he is keen to introduce us to favourite locations on his old beat, Leadenhall Market, built in 1881 at the cost of £99,000, and rather handsomely repainted and generally tarted up in the last few years. This used to be chop-house land — definitely a form of fast food, if only for the legendary celerity of the waitresses:

'The chop-houses are there for one purpose only: to feed financiers, press barons, captains of industry and lesser mortals (bowler hat, furled umbrella) during the frantic lunch-hour. The waitresses call you "dear", and serve you so fast they could probably fill a table four times in one hour . . .' (Adrian Bailey, *Food*, 1967)

Some of the City chop-houses survive, though most of the restaurants here are decided up-scale and far more leisurely. The market is crammed with expensively besuited men and women toying with lemon soles and unconventional rosé wines, lingering well into the afternoon office hours. But Peter tells us to be patient, for there are some unexpected nooks to be crannied.

As we wander, I mention the disparaging remark that our new Walthamstow-Turkish friend Chris made about Romania, which prompts Peter to a bizarre racist slur he once heard in a Turkish kebab place in Kent: 'Romanians? They eat grass.' Repeated in cold blood, the phrase strikes us as so odd that he writes it down in a notebook, for possible deployment in a future poem. Then we catch up with Richard, who's hit pay dirt: a sushi joint.

If sushi is not the healthiest of fast foods (though I strongly suspect it may be) it is surely the most beautiful. We have been planning to photograph some in the right location all along, and this new-ish outlet is perfect, partly because since it displays all its myriad varieties of lunch boxes on easy-access metal shelves: a small library of raw fish and rice confections — Japanese. They seem mildly puzzled by our interest, but willing enough to let us shoot away.

There is an idle assumption among xeno-phobes that raw seafood is a radical innovation on the British food scene, and that sushi is the vilest of all vile foreign muck, to be spurned by all free-born Englishmen. But is the moment of daring involved in one's first-ever bite really all that different from the challenge faced by gener-ations of pint-sized Cockneys when first presented with a laaaahvly plate of cockles and whelks? Which leads us to:

CRUSSH BAR
CORNHILL, EC2

The weather is uncomfortably hot today, so we decide to combine research and refreshment by sampling the wares at this new-ish juice bar, which first caught our attention because of its interesting back room — a sort of snug area, mildly reminiscent, albeit without the statues of naked girls, of the Korova Milk Bar from Stanley Kubrick's version of Anthony Burgess's novella, *A Clockwork Orange*. This sets me to pondering . . .

→
More raw fish at **Yo! Sushi**, *p.133*

→
More juice at **Crussh**, *p.117*

ON THE RISE AND FALL OF THE MILK BAR

An unusual instance of a fast food institution that came into being more or less in response to a Government initiative, the British Milk Bar was born in 1935. (Two years earlier, the government had set up the Milk Marketing Board.) Loosely inspired by American soda fountains, and dressed up with chromium plating and high bar stools, the milk bar encouraged young people to glug plenty of the nutritious fluid in the sugar-adulterated form of milkshakes.

The earliest example — the Black and White — opened not so very far from here at 54 Fleet Street on 1 August 1935, and it stayed open 24 hours a day, partly to slake the non-alcoholic thirsts of London's newspapermen. Emulators soon followed, and at the height of the boom there were some thousand branches around the country. In many provincial towns, the local milk bar provided just about the only evening alternative to the pub, the fish and chip shop, or the parlour. Richard Hoggart wrote a famously disgusted passage about the 'peculiarly thin and pallid form of dissipation' they offered, but by that time they were already in decline. Burgess's Korova Milk Bar was an inspired leap of imagination to a future when the drinks in such bars would be laced with amphetamines and hallucinogens; it also served to hint at the fundamentally infantile taste of its hoodlum anti-hero, Alex — a big, murderous baby.

Milk bars may be largely a thing of the past, but juice bars appear to be springing up all over. Apart from the encounter at Nin Com Soup, this is my first direct experience, and though the prices are a touch on the steep side, I'm rapidly becoming a convert. My 'Fat Blaster' — a combination of juices and so-called 'boosters' (the full Crussh range includes Ginseng, Spirulina, Guarana, Bee Pollen, Echinacea and Aloe Vera) — slides down the throat with a coldness that is just this pleasurable side of painful, and the fruity, sugary-acid flavours cut right through the nasty City-smoke taste in my mouth. It almost makes you shudder. Given a big enough expense account, I could probably drink several pints of this chilly refreshment.

Pete tells us that, as far as he's aware, the first chain of juice bars in London was opened in the early 1990s by one of his ex-students, a bloke from Gerrard's Cross who soon grew rich on the proceeds . . . but his story is interrupted by the arrival of a young woman called Jo, who is publicity manager for the Crussh chain and wants to know what (she doesn't quite say 'the hell') we are up to.

Once it's established that we are innocents, her initial suspicion gives way to an enthusiastic sales pitch. The Crussh chain, she tells us, started in business *c.*1998, and there are now nine branches around the capital, including two in Docklands and one at the ever-expanding BBC centre in White City. The main appeal to customers is the health kick — 'healthy food, but fast' — though that rational attraction is reinforced by the calculatedly swanky design of the bars, each of which is different. We really need to see them for ourselves, she says, and hands us a list.

Somewhat intrigued, we proceed in an Easterly direction (via the DLR) to check out the:

CRUSSH BAR

There is a strange decorative detail on the counter, near the till: a miniature lawn. Except that it is not a decorative detail. It is the raw material for one of the Bar's most heavily promoted heath-boosting products: Acai, pronounced ah-sai-ee. This, it seems, is much favoured by Dockland workers first thing in the morning, especially if they've had a heavy night on the lager. Yes, Gentle Reader: 'They Eat Grass.'

So we will have to try some, too. Heidi, the South African woman at the counter, performs the ritual. She cuts a portion of grass with nail scissors; feeds it slowly into an old-fashioned, hand-cranked metal meat grinder. A dry-ish, pale green, turd-like substance comes out of the large hole to the left; a slender trickle of dark green juice falls from a smaller hole into a plastic shot glass. When three shot glasses are filled, we chug them back, and then bite into slices of apple to kill the taste. Which really needs killing: grass tastes pretty much like it used to taste when you were a little kid and wondered why something so pretty wasn't also edible. Vile.

'Soylent Green,' says Pete.

The thing costs £1.50 a shot. According to the propaganda, it is packed with stuff that will make you live forever: '. . . the highest density of naturally occurring antioxidants of any food on the planet' (I question the term 'food'), and it 'contains high levels of essential fatty acids omega 6 and 9 . . .' (thank God for that). What's more, 'the cultivation and harvest of this fruit actively helps to protect the Amazon rain forest from the threat posed by ranchers and loggers'. So, once again, it can make you smug as well as healthy. Even so, it still tastes like muck. I order a pineapple smoothie to take away the residual insult to my palate.

CRUSSH BAR
JUBILEE PLACE, DOCKLANDS

This is deserted. Apart from the goodies we have seen at the other Crussh bars, it also sells bottles of what is alleged to be miraculously health-giving water, which has been tampered with at the molecular level so as to banish all fatigue. Indeed? I have some snake oil you might be interested in, too. Pete offers to buy me one, but the better part of two quid for a bottle of lukewarm water is a joke I can live without.

BAGEL FACTORY
JUBILEE PLACE, DOCKLANDS

This is also deserted. Pete observes that, in its clinical solitariness, it makes Edward Hopper's definitive evocation of modern urban loneliness, *Nighthawks* (an image you see everywhere in London these days — a legacy of the recent Hopper retrospective at Tate Modern) look positively clubby and cosy.

A silver plaque spells out, again, the sales pitch to health:

Why bagels?
Low in fat
High in energy
Perfect fuel for Living!

A nagging health-scare statistic at the back of my mind tells me that an average bagel is a damn sight more fatty than regular bread, but the part of the slogan that seems most unappetizing is the word 'fuel', even though it is a metaphor I don't mind using myself. Do customers really like being reminded that they are soft machines?

BIRLEY SALT BEEF BAR
CANARY WHARF

This is closed, but the wildly eclectic range of posters, signs and objects on display makes it a magnet for any photographer or amateur semiotician. I am particularly struck by a large poster of frolicking cartoon pigs: 'We support compassion in world farming.' Pigs for a beef bar? The African security guards move in as Richard shoots Birley's red neon sign, and rapidly establish that we have no permits. We are firmly escorted off the premises via a circuitous route which takes in a Japanese place, Itsu, we'd been hoping to snap because of its cute monorail service of dishes and inventive mobile decor — Victorian stained glass as re-imagined by Alexander Calder. The security guards stick with us all the way to the station entrance. We wave them goodbye. On the way out of Canary Wharf, I am struck by the slogan for a branch of the Tex-Mex chain Chili's, and briefly consider it as a possible epigraph for this project:

GET IN, GET OUT
AND GET ON
WITH YOUR LIFE

Food thus not part of life? It's time for some cold, cold lagers, and some slow, slow food. We find the latter in an Italian restaurant in Soho, where the Polish waitress serves us rare lamb cutlets and talks to us enthusiastically about the giants of her country's cinema, and particularly Andrzej Wajda's nationalist epic, *Pan Tadeusz*.

RAINY HOURS IN SOUTHALL

Right from the start of our mission, we've known that sooner or later we'd have to pay a visit to Southall, Asian capital of Middlesex, shared — not always harmoniously — between Muslim, Sikh and Hindu settlers, with a more recent sprinkling of refugees from Somalia. Not many of us white folk make the brief journey here from Central London, a neglect which is daft, or unimaginative, or worse, because Southall's superficially dowdy appearance (a deeply English suburban dowdiness, pierced here and there by the odd golden minaret, dazzling even in the drizzle) is deceptive: it has a lot to offer. What we didn't expect was that when we arrived the rain would be bucketing down with a vengeance, making the place even less seductive than usual. Shoulders hunch, collars turn upwards, a thousand umbrellas bloom, the gutters back up into puddles which the buses then send flying in drenching sheets.

Once in a while, the rain eases off to a mild drizzle, but it's still unpleasant enough, particularly for Richard, who today has opted to wear a light shirt and no jacket, the foolish optimist. Spirits low, we cast the primary mission aside for an hour or two and decide to go for a proper sit-down lunch.

ROXY NEW ASIAN TANDOORI RESTAURANT

SOUTHALL

Like Gaul, the Roxy is divided into three parts: a bright, bustling fast food zone where the staff serve up takeaway snacks and Indian sweets at high speeds; a more sedate lunch area, where Sikh businessmen in sober grey suits and sombre turbans talk quietly as they munch their breads and pulses, washing the hot food down with draughts of water from metal flagons; and a much fancier restaurant-cum-bar for the evening trade, where the tabletops have white marble Lazy Susans and the flattering lighting would make the plainest courting couple look a little bit glitzy.

Richard and I are the only pale-faced Northern Europeans here just now, but no-one makes us feel as if our presence is an ill-judged impertinence, or anything out of the ordinary: indeed, once we've polished off a huge lunch (£21 total for stomach-distending piles of chicken bhuna, bhindi, fish curry, naan, pilau rice, plain rice — all delicate, fresh and non-greasy), the manager invites us to hang around as long as we like: 'Treat this place as if it were your own home . . . even the kitchen, if you like. We are very, very clean.' So they are: the lavatories would probably win awards for hygiene and colour-coordination. And he plies Richard with quantities of 'jalbee' — some stores are calling it 'jalebi' — that crispy, orange-coloured sweetmeat that's made from syrup and looks a bit like short lengths of tangled rope.

Fired up by his chicken bhuna and an unusually open invitation, Richard starts snapping away in the fast food zone. His willing model here is Mr Harjinder Singh, whose bright red turban is like . . . well, like a red rag to Richard, who dotes on his primary colours. Harjinder is a natural model, unselfconscious and responsive to direction, though it seems as if he's not much of a judge of accents.

'What country you come from?' he asks Richard.

'Urr . . . well, Cambridge.'

'Funny. You sound Indian.'

Attuned to the presence of deities by our protracted experiences with icons of Princess Diana, I notice that the sweet counter is presided over by the image of a beatific sage.

'Obviously a very holy man?' I propose to the manager.

'Guru Nanak,' he explains, 'Our God.'

I suspect that some theological nicety has been lost in translation here, but the drift is clear enough, as is the image of Guru Nanak on another poster, where he takes his place among a pantheon arrayed in the sky above the Golden Temple of Amritsar.

When we leave, it is handshakes all round. 'Please come back, any time.' Far from impossible, sir.

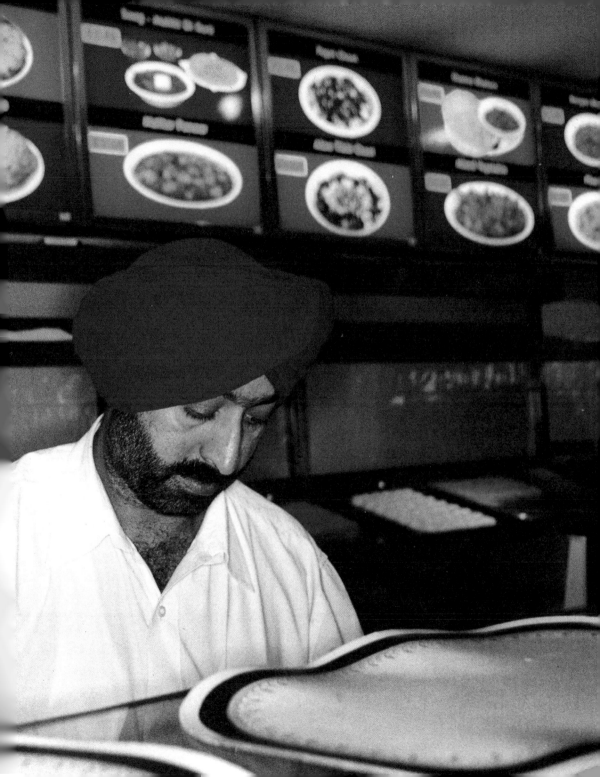

RAGHUVANSHI SWEETS
SOUTHALL

The walls of this colourful and fragrant emporium are covered with bright representations of assorted Hindu deities, some of them decked out with garlands of flowers: a cheering sight on this chilly, spirit-crushing day. I nod discreetly in the direction of Ganesha, vaguely remembering that he is the god you need to invoke when setting out on or already engaged in a long-term project. Well, it never hurts to be polite. The gentleman behind the counter wears his white coverall like a lab coat: he's about 60, slight and scholarly-looking. In other contexts, you'd take him for a gentle-mannered don. He is more than happy for us to photograph, and plies Richard with free sweets, notably a substance called 'Khoya Barfi', which Richard describes as being a bit like cheese in texture and mildly nutty in flavour.

I make a list of the delicacies on sale: Gol Gapa, Alu Wada, Kachori, Pholl Khaja, Boondi . . . Meanwhile, a burly, bearded man with mandala-like tattoos on the backs of his hands comes in and places his order for a bulging plastic bag full of sweets. He looks suspiciously at both of us, particularly at Richard, who is still stuffing his face with free sweeties.

'What you think of that?' Tattoo guy asks him.

'Very nice,' Richard splutters through his Khoya Barfi. 'Delicious.'

'Yeah,' says Tattoo Guy grimly. 'Yeah, they all say that.'

(We do not need to be told who 'they' are. We are they. This could turn ugly.) Tattoo guy goes on: 'You ask, how do you like the Indian food, the Indian sweets, and they say, oh, lovely, really, really nice . . . Then, five minutes later, they call you Paki.'

Uh-oh.

I whizz through my mental files for some appropriate response, find none. Hard to say anything that won't sound priggish or cod-innocent, except maybe 'Am I my [bigoted] brother's keeper?' (Possible answer: yes, you are. And don't come round here again until you've put your house in order, mate.) But there's no need for us to say anything, because the manager is clearly agonized by embarrassment at this mild flash of racial tension, and speaks up on our behalf 'Oh no, no, there are all sorts of people, really, all sorts — good people, bad people . . .'

Despite his disgruntlement, Tattoo Guy agrees to pose for a couple of shots. As he leaves, I offer my hand for shaking, and say thanks for his time and trouble. Slightly to my surprise, he accepts it, and all but winks as he goes out the door. 'Don't take things too seriously,' he tells me. The manager is so keen for us not to go away with ruffled feathers that he plies Richard with still more sweets and fizzy drinks, and simply will not take any money for it.

Note for connoisseurs of ethnic stereotypes: from now on, every establishment we enter in Southall insists on giving us free food and drink. I hazard that it's partly because, defining ourselves as guests, of a sort, rather than customers, we must be given full family hospitality. I'm sure that Tattoo Guy would point out that benign racial clichés are hardly less pernicious than the hostile kind, but the next time someone talks about Asian traditions of generosity, I plan to nod in agreement.

→

More Indian sweets at **The Shahenshah**, *p.131*

ASIAN KEBAB
SOUTHALL

ROSHNI
SOUTHALL

'This,' Richard proclaims, 'could really be in the Third World.' He means that the outlet onto the street is a shack-like assemblage of plastic, cheap wood and cheaper metal, the signs are all hand-scrawled, and occasional bursts of flame leap up and out from the grills at the back. It's far too cramped for both of us to go in, so I wait on the street, and within seconds am accosted by a short young man in a natty suit.

'You from Health and Safety?'

Far from it.

And I explain our mission. Sunil, for such is his name, hits me up for a few quid's worth of sponsorship for his NSPCC Bungee Jump, and then gives me his personal take on Southall, where he's lived all his life. The various communities are getting along reasonably well at the moment, he thinks, but 'the drugs, mate. You wouldn't believe it. I'm telling you . . . crack, heroin . . .' I point around at the shoppers, the matrons and the grandfathers and the schoolgirls, who look almost boringly respectable to me. 'Yeah, yeah, to the untrained eye. But it's desperate. The young people, they got nothing to do, so they get into drugs.' I have no idea whether Sunil is slandering his manor or if this is the harsh reality; nor do I have any idea whether his NSPCC thing is a scam. I don't care all that much, either: this is the kind of jaundiced corrective we need today, when everyone except Tattoo Guy is being so impossibly nice to us.

Richard emerges, hot and flustered but definitely fired up. 'There's this dish they were making — it looks amazing — you've got to come with me and work out what it is, I couldn't understand them.' So, with the help of a lot of sign language and a menu card, we finally work out the name of the exotic dish which has so excited Richard's eye.

It translates as 'Kebab Roll'.

Let us admit it: this place is really more of a sit-down restaurant — quite a posh one, at that — than a fast food place, but we are both entranced by its unique water feature: a tall, vertical tank of brightly illuminated, violently churning fluid. (It can't do much good for customers with queasy digestions.) Asam, the head chef, and his colleagues Balal and Ahmed pose for us with undisguised excitement. Do all restaurateurs secretly crave a career in showbiz?

THE SHAHENSHAH (100% PURE VEGETARIAN RESTAURANT TAKE AWAY AND SWEET CENTRE)
SOUTHALL

If not exactly a treat for the eyes — frankly, it's a bit gloomy and dingy and tatty at the edges — the Shahenshah more than compensates when it comes to the taste buds. This is a truly exceptional place; as a matter of fact, you could reasonably call it world famous, if you're attuned to the right culinary wavelengths, since vegetarian tourists from as far afield as Australia, Singapore and the USA have made a special digression out to Southall to sample its offerings, as lauded in dozens of veggie Good Food guides. Unmissable, the books say; and, anyway, as we are now both pretty well sodden, the chance of staying in the warm and steaming ourselves a little drier is quite alluring.

Not many people are eating at the tables, but the trade in takeaways is unrelenting, and we don't want to get in the way. So, after a few diplomatic preliminaries, Richard nips behind the counter and plunges into the kitchen area, from where I can hear him flirting outrageously with three (or is it four?) generations of ladies: Asha, the matriarch, Rakhi (resplendent in brightest pink), Sita the chef, and Manjint and Parmjit the assistant chefs, all of them under the sagacious eye of a rather imposing woman — 'Grandmother'. (Hard to tell if her function is supervisory or familial; probably the latter, as Rakhi calls Asha 'the boss'.) It can't be altogether convenient for them to have Richard thrashing and gangling around in a fairly small preparation space, but before a few minutes have passed I hear the all-too-predictable noise of feminine laughter. Oh, they like him all right. Photographers, eh? What's their secret?

Left out alone in the body of the restaurant, I sip my (free) coffee and look across the rainy high street to the Himalaya Palace Cinema, an extraordinary exercise in dragon-festooned Chinoiserie which (I'm guessing here) gives every appearance of dating back to the 1920s or so, and has been modified for its new Asian clientele. Now showing: Yash Chopra's *Veer-Zaara*. My compensation for waiting on my lonesome comes in the form of a sample hot samosa. If you're used to the kind of samosa where the spud comes in hard little cubes or shapeless lumps, this is a revelation: the crisp pastry shell is filled with light, airy, cunningly spiced mashed potato. Instant oral gratification. I feel somewhat cheerier.

Eventually Richard has his quota of shots and we are sent on our way with loud good wishes, demands that we come back soon and still more free sweets. I pump Richard for details of what he's seen, and he speaks in almost awed terms about the way in which the women have coordinated their various acts of baking and cooking, clearly knowing exactly how much time it needs for a pastry to swell, a pulse to soften, a spice to yield flavour. (In retrospect, I suspect that he didn't use quite such flagrantly erotic terms.) All that, and they kept joking with him throughout, silver-tongued devil that he is.

We came out here to Southall this morning the slow way, via the Central Line and local buses: a good couple of hours in all, though instructive ones. We opt to take the mainline train back into Paddington and (since I doze off immediately) appear to be there in two minutes flat. My mental map of London has been rearranged today, and decidedly for the better: at the very least, I can definitely envisage nipping up to Southall for a pleasant evening out with the neighbours.

In short, Southall has left a good taste in the mouth.

$\rightarrow$

English ethnic pastry at **West Cornwall Pasty Co.***, p.140*

YO! SUSHI
PADDINGTON STATION

An interesting case of natural vision vs camera vision: unaided by 35mm or 50mm lenses, the eye sees the Yo! Sushi stand, with its cute miniature railway chugging little dishes around in an endless loop, as bright and cheery and maybe just a little bit on the glamorous side. But, as Richard soon confesses, it is an absolute bastard to photograph adequately, especially if you don't want to violate the peace and privacy of the early evening munchers. The staff, given the OK over the phone by their manager, are obliging enough, and let Richard squirm and crouch and contort himself around them as they dice and slice and arrange their delicacies, but I can tell that he's frustrated. He cheers up a bit when Anneka, one of the staff, takes her meal break and poses for him with chopsticks at suggestive full port.

Out of nowhere, a nasty little incident: an Asian kid, twenty-ish, scruffily dressed and (odd detail) smoking a cigarette which is burning from the middle instead of the end, grabs hold of the tips jar and starts to make a run for it. Two or three of us move in to block his path, and the young Korean woman who is acting manager fearlessly grabs the jar back. But instead of hoofing it, the kid remonstrates loudly, actually whining plaintively about the injustice of it all as though we had hurt his feelings, and even tries to negotiate some of the coinage back. When this doesn't work, he stomps off petulantly, grumbling to himself, and then — why? why? — slinks back with a glossy magazine he's just stolen and hands it to me: 'Here, you might wanna read this.' And he disappears again.

Richard polishes off the last of his shots. One of the diners, who has watched the whole incident, asks me if I plan to keep the magazine. I give it to her gladly.

$\rightarrow$
*A raw fish finale at **Caviare House**, p.140*

MICKY'S FISH BAR
NORFOLK PLACE, PADDINGTON

A small blue and white flag behind the counter proclaims the Greek provenance of this chippie, which is very much in the classic mode I remember from my childhood. (It's not inconceivable I may once have been brought here in my childhood, as Micky's has been in business for 42 years now). There are three Greek blokes cooking and serving. They call themselves George, Nick and George. Micky is not in evidence: maybe Micky was a myth. Business is thriving.

A cutting from *Now* magazine, stuck in the window, makes the implausible claim that it was at this very shop that Michael Jackson developed a taste for our national dish. It says that he used to nip down from a nearby hotel and load up with armfuls of the hot stuff. When younger George takes a break and wanders outside for a breath of non-fatty air, I point out the cutting and ask him what he thinks. He shrugs. 'I don't believe it.'

THE VAULTS
BELOW LONDON BRIDGE STATION

Richard is on another mission, something to do with hot rods (rather than hot dogs) in Sweden, so I decide to make today's solo journey a modest one. Anyway, we're both showing signs of wear and tear, too much fast food being bad for the brain as well as the body.

The once sinister area underneath London Bridge Station has changed dramatically. It's yet another sign-of-the-times outburst of healthy fast food — stand after stand, each one selling fresh fruits, nuts, juices and soups-on-the-spot and (less healthy, but comparably priced) posh chocolate. Embarrassed for life-lengthening choice, I opt pretty much at random for a deli-style place called Wendell's, and buy a turkey panino with chilli jam and roquette. £3.50, again.

Quite nice. Well, the chilli jam is tasty enough, anyway: someone, somewhere with a degree in biochemistry and a cushy grant must have analyzed the curiously, counter-intuitively harmonious marriage of hot and sweet flavours in certain cuisines. But break these few ingredients down into their basic functions and what you essentially have is a cold, posh kebab, in which the meat doesn't taste of all that much, and certainly doesn't gush with wicked, savoury juices. I feel that our fast food mini-odyssey is starting to come full circle.

DALLAS CHICKEN AND RIBS
NEAR VAUXHALL UNDERGROUND

Here they drink and there they cram
Chicken, pasty, beef and ham,
Women squeak and men drunk fall.
Sweet enjoyment of Vauxhall.*

Long hours of brooding, as so often of late, on the endlessly fascinating subject of the kebab has led me to consult my staggeringly learned friend and brother 'pataphysician, Robert Irwin, novelist and Arabic scholar. (Recommended works of scholarship: *Islamic Art* and *A Companion to the Arabian Nights*. Recommended novels: *Satan Wants Me, Exquisite Corpse*.) As usual, Robert is almost lethally busy, and on the brink of flying off to some conference in Syria or Tierra del Fuego on fourteenth-century *grimoires* or what have you, but he generously spares me a half-hour or so in the late afternoon, as the sun goes down. Tall, ramrod-backed and neatly bearded, he marches vigorously through the streets of Vauxhall as if crossing an Oxford quad or a Cambridge court.

Had we been following the pleasure principle, Robert's venue of choice, he says, would have been one of the several excellent tapas bars which have started to thrive in his neighbourhood, thanks to a recent influx of immigrants from Portugal and South America. This is a tempting option — I am very partial to a dish or so of *patatas bravas, bacalao, chorizo* or *pulpo*, well lubricated with Rioja or Galician beer — and Robert tries to twist my arm still further with learned nuggets about the history and philosophy of tapas, many of them gleaned from Alicia Rios's article in the *Oxford Companion to Food*.

*Anonymous early nineteenth-century ballad on the Vauxhall Pleasure Garden, which survived until 1859.

VAGUELY ON TAPAS

My favourite tapas joint, which I will not be naming here since it is quite small and far too many people already know about it, is in that raffish part of West London some wits have called No'Way — North of the Westway. By accident rather than premeditation, the mood of this Spanish-owned, Spanish-run place has wound up being faintly 1950s bohemian, and the clientele a unique mixture of locals (mainly, well, Spanish), loyalists and layabouts. I have never gone there without sooner or later falling into discussion with a painter, a musician, a Shamanistic therapist or an affable drunk. Some of the regulars are famous, one or two are mildly famous, and a lot more simply act as if they were famous. I curbed the regularity of my visits a few years ago when I realized how much of my time and income it was eating up to go there every night; but if tapas is fast food, then this Spanish outpost in No'Way is, I suppose, my favourite fast food place anywhere in the world. *Dos cervezas, por favor.*

But I resist the Great Vauxhall Tapas temptation, since Robert has also mentioned a classically unappealing fried chicken joint, just a few streets away. As we walk there, he fills me in rapidly on a few points worthy of consideration. In the Middle East, for example, it is usually much healthier to eat in the street than in restaurants: you can see the food being cooked freshly before your eyes. One reason for the difference in our respective culinary traditions is that Northern Europe was for centuries heavily wooded, and thus super-abundantly supplied with fuel, which allowed for slow and wasteful forms of cookery such as large-scale boiling, baking and roasting. With far less wood at hand, the Middle East naturally favoured frying and grilling.

Then Robert starts spieling out the references and the footnotes pell-mell: to a tome called *Culinary Cultures of the Middle East*, (ed. Sami Zubaida and Richard Tapper, I.B. Tauris, 1994), and particularly an essay entitled 'The Meyhane or McDonald's? Changes in Eating Habits and the Evolution of Fast Food in Istanbul' by Holly Chase. (I really must look this up some time.) He asks if I've thought about the Futurist cookbook of Marinetti and Co? (I have, and decided that despite their addiction to speed, this doubtfully edible cuisine of ball bearings and violet leaves did not really fit the bill); he laments the sorry habitués of a South London KFC branch ('the driftwood of life. Lonely, shabby, deformed'); he identifies 1951 as the earliest date recorded for the term 'fast food' in the United States (see C. Maryani, *The Dictionary of American Food and Drink*); he passes on, from his wife, an allusion to a scene in Dorothy Richardson's novel *Pilgrimage* in which the heroine sits in a Lyons Corner House, worrying about her weight and scrupulously eating only half her portion; he suggests I browse Eric Hobsbawm's autobiography for references to the government-backed 'British Restaurants' of the Second World War; he expatiates on the history of the Marmite factory just nearby; and he defies me to work an allusion to *The Anatomy of Melancholy* into the published text of this book.

By this time, we are at Dallas Chicken and Ribs. I hand over £4.75 for two pieces of chicken and an order of ribs, and we wander to a scruffy piece of open land to try it. The chicken is . . . well, just about edible for the genuinely hungry. The ribs are perfectly disgusting; by a good margin the most unpleasant foodstuffs I have encountered in this trip: a paltry layer of grey, fatty generic meat on a softened bone, slathered in a reddish sauce that tastes like heavily sugared battery acid. I force down one rib in the interests of social science, offer another to Robert (who winces and gives up after one bite) and bin the remainder. Robert wanders off home to pack for his conference and re-read Ibn Khaldun or whatever, and I am left alone and hungry in the Vauxhall wasteland. Time to go home.

WEST CORNWALL PASTY CO.
KING'S CROSS STATION

Who ate all the pies? I did, I did. A medium sized 'traditional' pasty costs £2.50 and it is served very, very hot — almost too hot to eat at first except in tentative nibbles. George Melly, in his highly entertaining memoir *Owning Up*, reminisces about the days when he toured the country as the singer in a poorly paid jazz band, and evokes the fierce, animal pleasure of stopping off at a snack stand on a cold night and biting into the painfully hot beef, chicken, or cheese and onion pies that were just about the only form of nocturnal sustenance available in a country that always closed down by eleven at the latest.

These pasties aren't in that league, or maybe I'm just not as cold and desperate as an itinerant jazz-man of the 1950s, but they are, as I know from previous trials here, pretty satisfying. An acquaintance who works in the city as a Risk Manager, whatever the heck that is, says that his commute home in the late evenings has in recent weeks been transformed by the advent of this pasty stand, which provides guaranteed mouth-pleasure after a long day of managing, er, risk. Let us see.

Hmm. Well, the meat content of this particular confection is lenten: minus point. On the other hand, the spicy tang of its gravy soaks right through the thin slices of spud and onion which make up the bulk of its innards. I eat it to the last fugitive crumb of pastry, consider that I have had a fair £2.50-worth of grub, and save the bag for research purposes. It has a cartoon of a piratical figure about to inhale a pasty the size of an American football, and tells me proudly that the product is 'Handmade in Cornwall — Freshly Baked Each Day'. Would it really be so much the less tasty for being made in, say, Slough? Ditto for Yorkshire pudding, Spanish omelette, Kentucky Fried Chicken, French toast, Welsh rarebit, Baked Alaska . . .

Oh well. I find a seat on the next train homewards and fall asleep at once. Primary mission completed, if not accomplished.

CAVIARE HOUSE SEAFOOD BAR
HEATHROW AIRPORT

The fieldwork is finished, the writing-up yet to come: time for some modest yet apt celebration at far and away the priciest fast food unit I have ever visited. I polish off a plate of gravadlax and thinly buttered brown bread with disgraceful speed (it is time, more than time, to re-learn the civil habits of eating slowly). My partner Claire decides to pass on the tempting option of oysters, and goes instead for mixed sushi. We chase our light seafood snack with glasses of chilled Sauvignon Blanc. The thought of Coca-Cola as a beverage fit for adult palates seems more than usually grotesque.

Next stop: the United States of America — Fast Food Nation, heartland of the Western obesity epidemic, acknowledged birthplace of McWorld. Cheers.

Items may vary

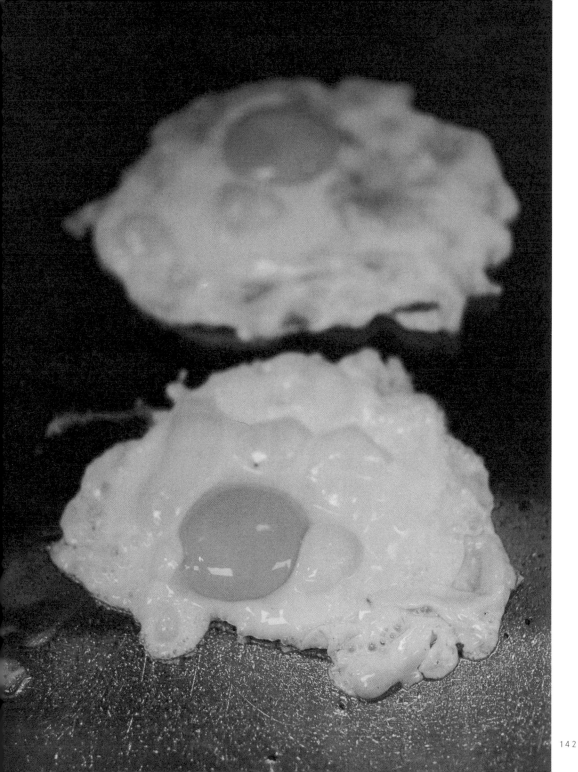

Brillat-Savarin, Jean-Anthelme
The Physiology of Taste
(translated by Anne Drayton from
La Physiologie du gout, 1825)
London, Penguin Classics, 1994.

Burnett, John
*Plenty and Want: A Social History
of Diet in England from 1815 to the
Present Day*
London, Nelson, 1966.

Burton, Robert
*The Anatomy of Melancholy:
A Selection*
ed. Jackson, Manchester, Carcanet/
Fyfield, 2004.

Carpenter, Peter
Choosing an England
Kent, Worple Press, 1999.

Clayton, Antony
*London's Coffee Houses: A Stimulating
Story*
London, Historical Publications, 2003.

Counihan, Carole and Van Esterick,
Penny (eds)
Food and Culture: A Reader
New York, Routledge, 1997.

Deighton, Len (ed.)
Len Deighton's London Dossier
Harmondsworth, Penguin, 1967.

Drummond, J.C. and Willbraham,
Anne
*The Englishman's Food: Five Centuries
of English Diet*
London, Pimlico, 1991 (Revised and
expanded from the first edition:
Jonathan Cape, 1939)

Elias, Norbert
*The Civilizing Process: The History
of Manners*
trans. Edmund Jephcott, New York,
Urizen, 1978. (From *Über den Prozess
der Zivilisation*, Basel, 1939.)

Fiddes, Nick
Meat: A Natural Symbol
London, Routledge, 1991.

Goody, Jack
*Cooking, Cuisine and Class: A Study
in Comparative Sociology*
Cambridge, CUP, 1982.

Klein, Richard
Eat Fat
London, Picador, 1997.

Levenstein, Harvey A.
*Revolution at the Table: The
Transformation of the American Diet*
New York, OUP, 1988.

Love, John F.
McDonald's Behind the Arches
New York, Bantam, 1986.

Mennell, Stephen
*All Manners of Food: Eating and Taste
in England and France from the Middle
Ages to the Present*
Oxford, Basil Blackwell, 1985.

Mintz, Sidney W.
*Tasting Food, Tasting Freedom:
Excursions into Eating, Culture and
the Past*
Boston, Beacon Press, 1996.

Oliver, Thomas
The Real Coke, The Real Story
New York, Random House, 1986.

Prendergast, Mark
For God, Country and Coca-Cola
New York, Scribner's, 1993.

Reiter, Ester
*Making Fast Food: From the Frying
Pan into the Fryer*
Montreal, McGill-Queen's University
Press, 1991.

Schlosser, Eric
Fast Food Nation
London, Penguin (paperback edition
with a new afterword), 2002.
(Originally New York, Houghton
Mifflin, 2001.)

Schott, Ben
Schott's Food & Drink Miscellany
London, Bloomsbury, 2003.

Steingarten, Jeffrey
The Man Who Ate Everything
New York, Knopf, 1997.

Steingarten, Jeffrey
It Must Have Been Something I Ate
New York, Knopf, 2002.

Tames, Richard
Feeding London: A Taste of History
London, Historical Publications, 2003.

Wallen, Martin J.
City of Health, Fields of Disease
Hampshire, Ashgate, 2004.

Watson, James L. (ed.)
*Golden Arches East: McDonald's in
East Asia*
Stanford, Stanford University Press,
1997.

Acknowledgements

Fast entered my life in the form of a surprise commission from Philip Dodd, who at that time was Director of the Institute of Contemporary Arts. The ICA had been working on various related projects in the broad areas of nutrition and health, under the general guidance of its Scientist-in-Residence, Dr Harry Rutter (who is also the Deputy Director of the South East Public Health Observatory): one of these was a study of fast food outlets in London, which included the production of an analytical map by Justine Fitzpatrick. Since then, the *Fast* project has mutated so often and so radically that its sober, scientific origins are now barely perceptible, but without Harry Rutter's work this book would never have existed, and he tells me that he would like to thank his colleagues:

Martin Caraher, Reader in Food and Health Policy, City University; Rachel Cottam, Director of Talks, ICA; Justine Fitzpatrick, Lead Analyst, London Health Observatory; Rob Henderson, Specialist Registrar in Public Health, L.H.O.; Bobbie Jacobson, Director, L.H.O.; Tim Lang, Professor of Food Policy, City University; Jenny Mindell, Deputy Director, L.H.O.

Dr Rutter, who has been kind and open-minded enough to give his full approval to the idiosyncratic paths that Richard Heeps and I have since walked, says that the work of this group will be appearing in assorted scholarly publications over the next couple of years.

Abbie Coppard was a sterling copy-editor of the original text.

My thanks to everyone who gave up time and potential income to join or aid our ramblings: Peter Carpenter, Leslie Felperin, Robert Irwin, Andrew MacDonald, Ray Sanger, Martin Wallen. Also to the usual peers and mentors for scholarship, advice and inspiration: Dr Susan Brigden, Alastair Brotchie, Dr Christopher Page, Dr Claire Preston, Rowan Routh, Iain Sinclair (*il miglior fabbro*), Peter Straus, Dr Peter Swaab and Clive Wilmer. And above all to everyone, named and un-named, who agreed to pose for Richard Heeps's photographs, let us hang around their places of work, plied us with foodstuffs or otherwise showed us generosity and tolerance.

Without Philip Gwyn Jones, *Fast* would have disappeared into the void; without Laura Barber (the Dorothy Parker of the e-mail), the task of preparing it for public life would have been much less hilarious.

Gratias ago.

KJ

My thanks to Natasha Heeps, Frances and Tudor Heeps, Sophie Belle, Nico Lyons, Liz Blackshaw, Nicky Adamson, Barry Grimward, Marshall Walker, Andy White, Paul Crompton, John Gregg, Jim Collett, Graham Magee, Martin Baxter, and Alice and David Aronshon.

RH